UNTANGLE THE WEB OF NARCISSISM

From Deceit and Chaos to Claiming Your Sanity

By Madison Frederick

UNTANGLE THE WEB OF NARCISSISM
From Deceit and Chaos, to Claiming Your Sanity

Inspired Legacy Publishing is a division of (DBA) Inspired Legacy, LLC
PO Box 900816
Sandy UT 84090-0816.

The material in this book is for informational purposes based on the author's experiences only and is not intended to replace medical advice. The content in some of the stories may trigger you in some way. If you feel you need further support at any point, please contact a licensed mental health professional.

ISBN 979-8-9878868-0-9 (paperback)
ISBN 979-8-9878868-1-6 (hardcover)

Printed in the United States of America.

What People Are Saying

"Madison models a great openness to the sometimes difficult process of growth and building the life you want."
-Kara Patin LCSW
Noble Soul Therapy

"Her raw honesty leads us through the journey of being raised by a narcissist, then married to one and how she broke free. She challenges us to bridge our suffering and move to a place of healing."
-Maryann I Colborn, Licensed Professional Counselor
Holistic Approach Mental Health, LLC

"From the depths of despair to choosing forgiveness and love."
- Kimi Avary, Relationship Navigation Specialist, Best Selling Author

"Emerging new Self-Help Author, Madison Frederick, hits a home run with Untangle the Web of Narcissism...This is a book worth reading over and over again."
-Polly Fletcher
Attitude Architect, Photographer & Artist

"I found the writing vulnerable, helpful, and very interesting content. There is so much to learn by reading this book."
-Ellen Havens ASN, BSN, CCTC

"The book provides hope without downplaying the challenging journey that is necessary to recover from the emotional and mental abuse inherent in narcissistic relationships."
-Karen Ann Bulluck
Bestselling Author, Speaker, Risk-Taking Coach
Daring to Transcend

"I especially liked that at the end of each chapter, Madison gave the reader the opportunity to see the steps to use."
-Wendy Turner, Salt Lake City

"Untangling" is part memoir, part self-help, but primarily it is informative. Wrapped in narratives of personal experience."*
-Kate Nash,
Language instructor, Bright Line Eating member

"Reading the "Untangle the Web of Narcissism" was written in a way that I could understand Narcissism."
-Judy Crenshaw

Acknowledgments

Writing this book was cathartic for me. There are many people I would like to thank, beginning with my son. Without the accusation declaring me a narcissist I wouldn't have begun my journey to discover why he said what he did. I am eternally grateful to him for his words. All the people who stood by me and supported me through this project. I would like to thank the book whisperer, Bridget Cook Burch, who gently guided me while I completed the manuscript. Without her love and encouragement, this book would not have been born. My editor, Hannah Lyon, and the whole staff of Inspired Legacy Publishing.

To my friends, in no particular order, Polly, Kathy, Kate, Mary, and Angie, who all offered valuable suggestions. My beta readers, you know who you are. My husband, John, supported me through all my crazies while writing when inspiration hit at all hours of the day and never once complained. Last but certainly not least God and His words of inspiration for the correct words to be written..

"The beacon of a lighthouse guides sailors
safely to shore.
My hope is that this book can serve
as your guiding light,
helping you find your way home
- home to your true self."

Madison Frederick

Table of Contents

Introduction

The behaviors I witnessed from my narcissistic dad began in my early childhood. They grew and festered just like bacteria in a petri dish. I adapted to these behaviors and perfected them on my own as a way to survive.

Why did I write this book? Because some people are blessed to live in an environment surrounded by parents and siblings who show kindness, love, and respect. They were accepted as they are. Their petri dishes didn't contain the pain and suffering that oozed into their lives resulting from abuse of all kinds, including narcissism and many of its accompanying nuclear fallouts of alcoholism, codependency, or other addictions.

Since you have picked up this book, I'm going to assume it was likely that *your* life may not have always been so peachy. Regardless of what cards you were dealt, you likely have felt the ramifications of narcissism and learned your own set of survival skills that may have grown into your learned behavior or limiting beliefs that you are ready to untangle.

Not only do I recognize your pain, I recognize your freedom, and I invite you to tap into your inner resilience that may be as faint as a whisper. There are ways to get through learned behaviors and misguided beliefs about yourself. Not only is it possible, it is powerful, but it will require deep and abiding honesty with yourself. That is the first step. The next is self-compassion. It is necessary to disentangle from twisted beliefs that narcissists bring into their relationships.

Learned beliefs and behaviors are exactly that: *learned*. There's good news and bad news to that. The bad news is that these behaviors may be deeply embedded inside. When you were in survival mode, the patterns you developed were all you knew. And yet there is another side of the coin—that learned beliefs and behaviors can be *unlearned*, and new behaviors can replace the old.

Learning to live in peace and harmony regardless of what cards I was dealt has been hard-fought and hard-won. You might not believe it, but I feel blessed to have lived such a life . . . *now*. You may have heard that situations or traumas don't happen *to* you but *for* you. For a long time, I didn't believe anything painful or as hard could have possibly happened *for* me—at least not in the beginning stages of my journey.

It wasn't until I performed an autopsy on my life that I could see things clearly. Viewing my life under a microscope, I saw the truth about how the influences of my not always stellar behaviors affected all my relationships. I saw all the cracks in the foundation of my life. The results were painful . . . and far-reaching.

My reason for writing this book is for you to gain life-changing awareness and clarity to such a degree that you can discover it is possible also to have peace and harmony.

Throughout this book, I write vulnerably. Please be aware there may be content in some of the stories that could be triggering for you. I have provided tools that helped me through some rough patches in my life. My disclaimer is that I do not have formal training in psychology or psychotherapy from any university. Still, I have a life full of experiences and amazing sorts of training in multiple healing modalities along with proven, practical tools that have helped me gather the wisdom I am passionate about sharing with you. From therapeutic practices to Twelve Step groups, from reiki to essential oils to laughter, in each chapter, I offer solutions that may be of great benefit to you, as they have been to me.

It's not been a cakewalk, enjoying a kettle of tea and crumpets, sitting in an English garden. Instead, I'm telling my story, including all the thorns and weeds, and hoping you can learn quickly and powerfully from my life lessons so you won't have to experience them, or at least to the degree and the years I did.

You see, I not only adopted beliefs spewed upon me by a narcissistic father, equally selfish stepmother and stepbrother, but these were exacerbated by the abandonment of my birth mother and my marriage to an alcoholic narcissist because his treatment of me was so familiar.

I developed survival behaviors over time and in layers: enabling, codependency, addiction, and acceptance of labels given to me by others. I even established a pattern of behavior that I could not see or understand until it was blatantly pointed out.

But here's the deal: I believe there is a defining moment along every person's journey where you declare "enough already!" and two choices are to be made at that time. Do you continue to let other people or situations call the shots? Or do you pull yourself up by the bootstraps and ask for help to heal the traumas you have gone through? Do you claim your freedom from the knots that have held you bound and tangled up inside for so long?

This book can give you powerful tools to take you to the other side of:

- Narcissistic friends and family
- Narcissistic personal tendencies
- Abandonment and neglect
- Emotional, physical, and sexual abuse
- Addictions of all kinds
- Codependent behaviors

As survivors, we have this in common: we were likely groomed to put up with gaslighting, to pretend abuse didn't exist, to deny our pain for others' benefit, to deny our own accountability eventually, and to remain a victim to life. Your story will naturally be vastly different from mine, yet I would imagine the deeper you read, the more alike you may find we are. I also trust the tools you find within these pages will serve you.

And while I can't promise you there won't be any more hurts and pain in your life, I can help you learn to take an honest look at any situation you might find yourself in. And recognize that the way out is *through* the messiness of human life and family and relationships where there is beauty, joy, and hope for a brighter future.

The best part for me is that I have been using many of these techniques in my growing arsenal of skills with coaching clients for over two decades and have seen their faces soften when they have a new perspective of the traumas endured. My approach is often different as I have blended some of the methods I've learned, providing excellent opportunities for the growth of men, women, and children. I know that with the plethora of methods offered, *some tools* or many of them will work for you–and marvelously so. In fact, to support you, I've included some of these tools in the appendix. I've also included some note pages in the back if you want to capture any thoughts/notes for yourself, or you can keep a separate journal too. If something hits a tender place in you…remember to breathe, put the book down for a few minutes and then come back to it once you are ready to do so. And remember, if needed, seek the help of a licensed professional to support you through the possible triggering or sensitive place.

And last but not least, I promise if you use these tools and tell yourself the truth, no longer living in victimhood or blame, you'll finally be able to forgive yourself, along with others, the possibility of living an extraordinary rest of your beautiful life!

So, are you ready? Let's pull out the microscope and the petri dish of you and your relationships. Let's be accountable. You are in for the ride of your life.

CHAPTER ONE

Email Bombshell

Rock bottom became the solid foundation on which I rebuilt my life.
—J.K. Rowling

R ight after my granddaughter was born, my husband and I purchased a house, and my son and his family moved in with us. They stayed with us for a few years. It was an amazing highlight of my entire life. Having his family as a part of my everyday existence was a dream come true. I adore my son, his wife, and my grandchildren.

When that beautiful little granddaughter was about three, I vividly remember feeling horrified, standing in the kitchen the day my son informed me that the normally curious child had discovered Tylenol tablets loose in my purse! In fact, she had just put one in her mouth until her mom had made her spit it out.

My mind was racing as he told me the news, and I was trying to wrap my brain around what he had said. I thought about how the kids were always in my daughter-in-law's purse, looking for candy and gum, and as a rule, my purse was generally put away.

"You realize she could have died because she found that pill?" he declared, quite upset.

Responding in a tone I later regretted, I said, "It was only one pill; I don't see the big deal."

As he left the room, I stood frozen in my thoughts. At that moment, I wanted to say something, *anything* else, but the words wouldn't come. So, I said nothing at all. Hands down, I did not handle the situation *or* my response appropriately.

At the time, I also felt justified in thinking it wasn't my fault, like I had in so many situations in my life, avoiding taking ownership of something I did or said. I had learned that it would make me appear weak if I backed down. And when I was weak as a child or adult in many situations, I'd been attacked. It wasn't safe to be weak–or so I thought. The startled look on my son's face made me realize I had messed up big time. All I could think of was, *oh shit, now what?*

Yet I couldn't back down! In the past, I had not spoken up on many occasions when I should have, and there were times when I should have kept my mouth shut and didn't. Though not nearly as severe, we continued to experience the butting of heads at times.

About one-and-half years after that regretful incident with the Tylenol, my husband John and I sat in the front room of our house in Maryland, enjoying a cup of coffee and checking our emails on our laptops like we usually did. That morning the sun was beaming through the window, offering us a sense of comfort from the world outside.

I was expecting an email from my dad, who was supposed to send me some information. Instead, I saw an email from my son, which struck me as odd since we usually communicated via text or phone call. Upon reading it, I felt like I had been punched in the gut. Seemingly out of nowhere, I was blindsided with harsh words on my screen. They declared: "*Madison, you are a narcissist!*"

I was stunned and confused. *He's never addressed me by my first name before; he's always addressed me as Mom.* His email continued, telling me he didn't want anything to do with me ever again, and that I would not be allowed to be part of his life or that of my two grandchildren.

I want to make myself clear on this point. I do not blame my son. I need to acknowledge, right here and now, that *I had a definitive part in creating this estrangement between my son and myself.* That accusation was an excruciating and beautiful catalyst for me to create who I have become today. There was a time that the pain felt so unbearable, but for the learning, I will be forever grateful.

In the email, my son also mentioned that John and I did many things for them that were unsolicited and unwanted, and there was always a price tag attached. In hindsight, I see how that was undoubtedly true. Unwittingly, having learned those old family patterns, I had secured an emotional price tag to things we bought or did for their family.

In a twisted way, I was looking for validation that my son loved me. I believe I cut the legs out from under him in doing so. He was an adult and I should have treated him as such. It would have been better for all of us if I instead had empowered him and let him be the man he had become. I didn't know what that meant with my limited knowledge at the time.

My son and his family *were* my world. So much of my life revolved around them and the joy my grandchildren brought me. I couldn't imagine life without them. I couldn't imagine a world where we didn't have contact, connection, hugs, celebrations of their rites of passage, and so much more.

At the time, my son provided a long list of examples showcasing how many times in my life I had said or done things that, to him, proved I was a narcissist. *What on earth prompted his words?* I asked myself. Even though I sat in the front room, as you can imagine, my entire foundation crumbled from underneath me.

My son's email said he had no interest in discussing the subject further, instructing me not to bother calling or responding because there would be no reply. He repeated his instructions a second time: "Do not try to contact me because there is nothing to discuss."

Tears streamed down my face as I tried to make sense of it. I tried relaying what I had just read to my husband but could not get the words out. My hands shook uncontrollably as I handed him my laptop. John's touch lingered on my hands, offering me comfort as he gently took the laptop from my grip.

When he was done reading, in a riled-up voice, my husband declared, "You're not like that at all, *and* to cut off all contact is unbelievable!" He protectively put his arms around my shoulders and pulled me close as I sobbed.

Feeling overwhelmed and defeated, all I could muster was, "I don't understand what just happened. I need to be alone," I finally whispered. "I want to lie down for a while. I can't think straight right now."

Back in our bedroom, I crawled under the covers and pulled the blanket over my head, shut my eyes, and prayed for sleep. I couldn't get comfortable no matter which way I lay. I tossed and turned, but the sleep just didn't come. With closed eyes, I could see the words, *"You're a narcissist"* pass through my mind repeatedly, as if I was watching the landscape zoom by while riding on a train that I couldn't control.

I thought about my accuser, and the phrase that came to mind was not a healthy one:

How dare he? We have grandparents' rights; we'll take them to court! In my mind, I was flipping him off. But just as soon, I realized I was furious, and that kind of lashing out at him was a knee-jerk reaction. Taking them to court was certainly not the answer and would probably make things worse. I continued to replay the accusation in my mind. I knew there wasn't anything I could do about it. I told myself I needed to let it go, but how was I supposed to do that? My world as I knew it had been destroyed.

Maya Angelou once shared with Oprah a profound thought that Oprah still shares with people today on her shows and network. Maya said, "When you know better, you do better." I was suddenly thrust into a hero's journey of learning *how to know better* so I could do better.

I tried to talk myself into letting it go and focusing on other, more positive things. That way, I could move on, or so I thought. Only I did what I always did in the past–buried my feelings.

I honored my son's request for no contact, as excruciatingly hard as it was.

In the meantime, I figured out a plan to volunteer my time serving others so I could move forward with the unexpected time on my hands generally spent with my grandchildren and their families. I did some work at Arundel House of Hope, a nonprofit center that provides services for the homeless population. My husband and I helped organize a week-long event at our church where representatives from various state and federal agencies assisted the homeless in signing up for services, i.e., replacing social security cards, applying for food stamps, and employment opportunities, among other things. It certainly kept us busy!

But even focusing on that direction, the words in that email continued to haunt me. As you can imagine, it was a very confusing time for me emotionally. I wasn't functioning well. I went into a very dark place. I started going to therapy to work through the pain. About nine months after beginning therapy, it was suggested that I check into a hospital's psych unit for a couple of weeks to sort things out and get some medication to help me.

With the help of therapy, I thought I could get my feet on the ground enough to function again. However, it was just a band-aid covering the pain I was feeling from the estrangement from my son and his family.

As the years rolled by, I continued blaming my son's email for my misery, not taking responsibility for my actions. And guess what? I know now that was a very narcissistic reaction! At the time, however, I didn't know a better way of living, thinking, or being.

Because of that experience, however, I began looking at my learned behaviors through different lenses. As a longtime personal development seeker, I identified my character flaws–and there were plenty. At first, I condemned them. After all, the ripple for me was hugely painful. By and large, however, I came to understand that character flaws are simply part of the human experience.

In my case, I developed the behaviors of enabling, codependency, blaming, and control issues for self-preservation, having been raised in a home with a horrifically narcissistic parent. These learned behaviors could, in fact, make it appear I was a narcissist. In fact, these behaviors through the years caused many problems in my relationships.

Along my journey, I was introduced to the world of Doterra, a local essential oils company, and the value they could add to my life. I soon learned that each oil performed differently, and sometimes in multiple facets. The oils boosted my mood, helped me stay focused, helped me sleep more soundly, relieved stress and anxiety, and helped me with headaches.

As part of my continuing healing, I began writing this book. It quickly became apparent that I needed to investigate the "label" narcissist I had been given. Afterward, I went on my arduous and miraculous journey, researching how such a narcissist would behave. I asked myself the question: *Am I a narcissist?* Did I indeed meet the qualifications?

I am in awe of the number of things I learned because of it, not only about myself but also about my entire family, including family dynamics and patterns and individual growth. None of that would have been possible without that bombshell. That's why I am eternally grateful for my son's accusation.

In retrospect, I understand my son was only doing what he believed was best for his family and acting like a responsible, protective parent. I am very proud of how he and his wife took action. Thinking about my granddaughter's safety and well-being was the primary concern. He wouldn't have sent the email if he didn't believe he had good reason.

Things to Consider

The growth I have been able to experience because of the miracle given to me by my son and by God is off the charts! Who knew how many life-changing blessings and inner transformations would come from one single label?

I have learned that having been raised by a narcissist, I developed narcissistic characteristics as a defense mechanism to protect myself. Finally, I learned that life isn't always about me being right. Next, I let go of my lingering anger so much that I could see why my son would think I was a narcissist. After all, during the Tylenol episode and plenty times before and after, I had not taken accountability for my actions. So now, I had two big takeaways from the situation I had found myself in:

- I used justification when I couldn't take responsibility for my words or actions.
- My son was only looking out for his family's well-being.

While your story is different, my deepest wish is for you to know that it is possible to learn and grow from your character flaws, bring extraordinary healing experiences, and bring greater accountability and joy into your relationships.

Because of my research, I wanted to know if I had learned narcissistic behaviors from my dad. I was looking for insight into my past. I was finally willing to put my life under the microscope. And while I still hope that sometime in the future, I may have the opportunity to reconnect and rebuild a healthy relationship with my son and his family, I also know that may never happen. I have continued with this book anyway, with the strong desire that the information opens your mind and heart to the effects of narcissism and how to heal from it to the extent you don't have to make the same mistakes—and that your life and relationships can be robust, healthy, vibrant, alive, and accountable.

CHAPTER TWO

He, Himself, and Him

The only principle that governs their minds
is the question, 'How do I look?
—Haruki Murakai

W*hy do I make excuses for them? I've done that all my life!*
I gave my dad and my first husband, Ron, chance after chance, hoping things would change. Narcissism has become a buzzword, proliferating online and used many times, although not understood by many. I didn't know at the beginning of this journey that I had been raised by a man who *was* one. I knew Dad was controlling and manipulative. I knew I simply couldn't please him—no matter how hard I tried, but a narcissist?

When I began, my quest and the memories of my life unfolded, I soon realized how big an impact narcissism had on my life and my relationships.

My Dad

Dad dominated and controlled my birth mother, Margaret, even to the extent that she had no say in what I would be named. She thought they had agreed to name me Julie Ann. The first time she heard Susan Mae was at the same time as everyone else during a church service two weeks after I was born. That was when the men in my church gave me a blessing and announced the name I would be called. She was heartbroken. That's how Dad rolled; he *always* had the last word and made sure he *always* got his way.

Ten years after receiving the email bombshell, I was seeing a therapist when I asked her to give me the honest truth—to tell me if I was a narcissist.

"If you were a narcissist, Madison, believe me, you wouldn't be here in a therapist's office, asking if you are one! A narcissist doesn't believe anything is wrong with themselves and doesn't hold themselves accountable for anything they do."

In researching narcissism, I found out that it was true. I dove into books, academic journals, and coaching websites. The diagnostic criteria listed in the DSM 5 (*The Diagnostic and Statistical Manual of Mental Disorders*) read:

"A preoccupation with fantasies of unlimited success, power, brilliance, beauty, or ideal love. A belief that he or she is special and unique and can only be understood by, or should associate with, other special or high-status people or institutions. A need for excessive admiration." May 16, 2018.

When doing an Internet search, I also found many lists or versions of what professionals and what others believe are traits of a narcissist. Some sources say there are nine behavior traits; others say something different, depending on which authority is speaking.

When reviewing my life, beginning with my early childhood, my licensed therapist took me through a method called eye movement desensitization and reprocessing therapy (EMDR).[1] While taking me through the process, she was able to help me unravel the threads of the emotional wounds and help me realize how being raised by a narcissist had shaped me so strongly.

Living with and being raised by a narcissist was the catalyst for all of my learned coping behaviors—and a stark realization that it wasn't always easy for others to be in a relationship with *me*.

My dad and my birth mother, Margaret, got a divorce when I was three, and Dad and I moved into my grandma's house. When I was five-and-a-half, Dad came home from work one day and asked me in a matter-of-fact voice, "How would you like a new mother?"

I found out he had already asked that woman he was dating to marry him. *And on top of that, I was expected to call her "Mom." Why even bother to ask me?*

Thinking back to the day he told me he was getting married, it was no wonder I felt rejected and unimportant. She was coming into my life anyway. I was getting a stepmother like it or not. Oh, and that was not the only surprise.

My dad hadn't bothered to mention that my new mom had a son who was two years older than me. I was excited and terrified when I discovered that I had a brother. I didn't get to meet my stepmom or stepbrother until the night before they were to marry. Since all four of us were going to dinner at a KFC restaurant, I thought maybe the night wouldn't be so bad. After all, it had been my favorite take-out place while living with my grandparents.

We arrived at the duplex where this woman lived, and I watched as a stranger with light brown hair in a bouffant style came to the car to meet me. Her lips were painted bright ruby red, she wore extra-large, clip-on earrings that looked like buttons, and she was wearing a white dress with a huge black polka dot skirt that flared out, just like what Cruella de Vil wore in the book, *101 Dalmatians*.

Immediately, I was taken aback, and I just stared at her, frightened. I didn't like Cruella's character because she was so mean to the dogs. I wasn't sure why I transferred those feelings to my new mom, whom I learned that night was named Gladys. Maybe it was because her bright lipstick made her smile look like it was pasted on, and I wasn't sure how I was supposed to feel.

A few minutes later, my new stepbrother Randy, wearing a gloomy look on his face, approached the car and plopped down in the backseat. Randy, with his brown, butch-cut haircut, wore a scowl on his freckled face and didn't look any happier about the whole situation than I did. We scooted as far apart as possible when he got into the car. I clung to my armrest, and he to his. Neither of us said a word the entire ride to the restaurant.

Dad did marry Gladys the next day, and I officially had a new step-mother and stepbrother. I was not prepared for the significance of this event. It would forever change my life.

I was confused about the whole upheaval of my life. I didn't want to call Gladys "Mom," but I didn't dare to contradict Dad, so I complied. From then on, she was Mom. Unfortunately, things got worse for me. Dad now had two more people to manipulate and control.

I wouldn't learn until later that doing everything I could to survive the narcissistic atmosphere I grew up in, a petri dish of unhealthy and toxic relationships, bred behaviors I'm not proud of and caused me deep heartache in the years to follow.

Characteristics of Dad's Narcissism

As a grown adult and doing my intensive research, I clearly saw many signs that pointed to a long list of my dad's narcissistic behaviors.

- He consistently controlled and belittled me and others to make himself feel superior. He often did this in front of family, friends, and neighbors to make the emotional pain and feelings of helplessness and brokenness more impactful. It was an added threat.
- Dad always needed to have what the neighbors or his brother had–only bigger and better, including a boat, a camper, a new car, and a piece of custom-made furniture.
- Dad behaved boastfully around others, especially in crowds.
- He so badly needed to be the big shot that he might give extravagant gifts to local leaders and those he felt had power while neglecting his family to an extreme degree.
- He led people to believe he'd graduated from the University of Utah and enjoyed telling people the "*U*" was his alma mater–having attended only for one semester.
- He was consistently full of rage and defensiveness anytime he thought he was being criticized or slighted.
- He always needed to have the last word and was *always* "correct." Any attempts to contradict him only ended badly–even dangerously. I and others learned to be silent and let him be "right."
- Dad often presented himself as a big shot with lots of money,

pretending to be something he wasn't. After Gladys passed away, he married someone who believed he had lots of money because of how he presented himself, but she divorced him quickly when she learned the truth. We nicknamed this wife "The Hurricane" because she came in and out of our lives so quickly.

My New Life in Hell

My new family rarely went anywhere because it was always too expensive. However, on one occasion, when I was seven, we drove an hour away to a small swimming pool called Black Rock, nestled in the foothills of the Uinta Mountains in Utah. That Sunday, we were going to have a picnic lunch and then go swimming in the afternoon. I didn't want to go because I was self-conscious about my swimming skills. I especially didn't want my parents to see how frightened I was of the deep end of the pool. Randy and my new mom both swam like fish.

My stepbrother and I had been taking swimming lessons for about a month. Randy was perfecting his diving skills, and I was primarily working on holding my breath under the water. I was determined to overcome my fear of the pool's deep end. When we arrived at Black Rock, I noticed that there weren't any tall chairs with lifeguards on the side of the pool to protect people from drowning. I assumed they weren't there because it was a Sunday.

Dad had been peppering me with orders to jump into the pool from the minute we arrived. He became increasingly impatient because I sat on the sidelines in a chair. It only made me more anxious and I silently prayed Dad would leave me alone. I should have known what would come next when I didn't respond to his orders.

Dad sneered at me and yelled, "Get up off that chair now!" His face turned red, continuing to bark at me in a stern voice. "Just get in the damned pool already!"

I tried to ignore him. I turned my head slightly and, out of the corner of my eye, saw him come over to me, taking giant strides. As he got closer, I could see precisely how red in the face he was. It was almost as if steam was escaping Dad's flared nostrils.

"Why did we even waste money on swimming lessons for you?" Dad shrieked. "You're just an ungrateful snot!"

Snot. I was taken aback by the word that came out of his mouth. He had never called me a snot before, unlike my stepmom, who seemed to relish the term as her favorite description of me.

I clung onto the arms of my chair, resisting his attempt to pull me up, but to no avail. I lost my balance when Dad grabbed me by the arm, pulling me toward the deep end. I didn't know what hurt more—my feelings or my arm that he held onto so tightly. I began wiggling, trying to escape his hold, but he had too firm a grip.

"I'm going to teach you a lesson!" Dad pinched his lips together but spewed his anger with his eyes. "You'll either sink or swim!"

"Please don't make me," I begged, my voice fading into my tears. "The water is too deep here!"

Dad was not deterred in the least. He pushed me more than threw me into twelve feet of water. Pure panic and terror set in as I flailed all around, imagining the worst. I gulped and choked on the water, making it challenging to scream for help. As long, long moments passed, I was sure I would drown that day.

Suddenly, out of the corner of my eye, I caught a glimpse of a woman rapidly swimming toward me. I felt her strong arms slip around my waist and was grateful to be pulled toward the pool's shallow end, slowly. There, in her red, white, and blue swimming suit, she gently sat me on the steps where I caught my breath. She softly wrapped her arms around my shoulders, comforting me.

"I'll be right back; just wait here a minute," she said soothingly as she handed me a towel.

I watched as the woman strode toward Dad, yelling at him. Pointing and shaking her fingers, she cried, "Why in the hell did you do that?"

"I was helping her learn to swim. She needed to go into the deep end to gain confidence!" he snapped back. I knew that defensive tone of voice; he was trying to justify his actions.

"You just traumatized that poor child. You should be ashamed of yourself!" the woman declared. Looking disgusted at my dad, she added, "if there were someone I could report you to today, I would!"

Raising his voice even louder, I noticed that Dad tried to sound superior to her as he countered, "*I* know what's best for my daughter, and I repeat she's okay."

But my rescuer just ignored him. Instead, she returned to me, squatting down on my level. In a reassuring voice, she said loudly, "You'll be okay. I don't think he will try that again–not with everyone else witnessing just what happened."

Then she looked into my eyes and smiled warmly before standing up to be with her group. She was beaming comfort all over my body as she did so, giving me courage. I smiled back at her and thanked her. I knew she was the guardian angel who came to my rescue that afternoon and had been there to save me.

Mom and my dad didn't bother checking on me. I couldn't believe Dad had done that. He chose to act as if nothing had happened. *How did he think he was helping me?*

I wrapped the towel tighter around my shivering body. All I could do was sit on the steps, feeling deflated, embarrassed, and alone, but grateful for that woman and knowing everyone had just witnessed my ordeal. I prayed we could just leave.

Dad didn't say anything during the whole drive home. What he *didn't* say spoke volumes. It was a pattern I knew well, and I knew later every conversation and slight would be aimed at me and my mom and Randy would join right in. It was clear how unimportant I was; others perceived him as he pretended to be.

Only as an adult did I come to understand that my dad wasn't capable of recognizing my feelings and my needs, or anyone else's, for that matter. His mental illness precluded him from having any empathy whatsoever. The world revolved around him and had to cater to his center of gravity.

What Were the Effects on Me of Being Raised by a Narcissist?

- I had low self-esteem.
- I couldn't trust any relationships, especially men.
- I doubted myself and my capabilities.
- I became a perfectionist.
- I always craved validation from other people.
- I had a hard time identifying my feelings.
- I was unable to set boundaries in any of my relationships.
- I put everyone else's wants and needs before mine.
- I was attracted to toxic people with whom to be in relationships.

Dad treated me like I had no voice when I became an adult. Even when it came to making decisions about my children, he always had criticism to add, disguised as a suggestion made with love. Even though I was furious with him on many occasions, I was confused about how I could be so mad and yet, at the same time, felt guilty for feeling that way.

Narcissism in a family can be like a contagious disease. Over time, I discovered how many of Dad's behaviors *I* learned and had picked up along my path. Fortunately, I would come to understand that there were ways to protect myself and that there were *ways out of the insanity*.

It wasn't until my late thirties that I finally found the courage to stand up to him; it was the *only* way I could find my freedom from Dad's abuse.

Everyone has narcissistic traits to some degree. When someone takes pride in an accomplishment and speaks about it, it can appear to someone else that the person is boastful or thinks they are better than someone else. At times, people may jump to that conclusion because of their own insecurities or low self-esteem.

Some people are selfish by nature and may be motivated to do things unethical like cheating by nature, but that doesn't necessarily make them narcissistic. A narcissist is not only egocentric; they consistently disregard the feelings of others in their actions, their speech, and in their relationships. They have grand expectations of what others are to do for them but not what they are to do for others–except for that most profound need for their praise. The belief is everyone *must* think they are wonderful, regardless of what is happening behind closed doors. Appearance is everything to a narcissist.

When it comes to my children, I now understand how the learned behaviors I accumulated and what I inflicted on them was my attempt to have a close family. I believed the only way to create such an environment was to set "guidelines' for everything. I did not realize it was a control technique I learned and then used under the guise of parenting.

When I was sixteen, I promised myself not to be like my dad when I became a parent, yet that's precisely what I did. My parenting was done out of my love for my kids. Unfortunately, it was not received that way.

As a parent, I acted like the hall monitor at school, watching for anything out of line so I could quickly correct what I judged were disruptive behaviors from my children. This included making noise while playing, as children do in a doctor's office. The truth was, my self-esteem was so low at the time, I went out of my way not to be seen and didn't want my children's behavior to draw attention to us. I believed I would be judged as being a bad mother because I couldn't control them. I needed to control any and every situation. It was how I kept my family "safe" and acceptable in my eyes.

Finally, as I was learning about all the behaviors of a narcissist, I became saddened when I thought about all the times I justified my actions, just like my dad did. It isn't always easy, even now, with all that I have learned to avoid slipping into a justification for my actions and blaming other people when my life starts "life-ing." I get out of it faster now, but I never knew how to back down. I was taught it would make me appear weak if I did. Fortunately, I'm still a work in progress as I've discovered is true for every other human.

Because a narcissist raised me, I learned I had no sense of control or any semblance of self. Until I did this deep dive into my life, I had no idea that growing up in a narcissistic home would have such a profound impact on my life and that of my children and grandchildren.

The effects of being raised by a narcissist can have many consequences, as demonstrated in the list above.

In thinking about all the conversations I had with my dad, or all of the times he told me his opinion, I usually reacted in my mind with, "yes, but . . ." The "yes buts" always went unsaid.

Taking a stand for myself and redefining what I would or wouldn't put up with from him was a massive step. I didn't realize it at the time, but I had to draw a line in the sand to break ties with a narcissist to become my person.

Untangling a Narcissistic Relationship

Ultimately, this process entails standing in your power and realizing that you are in charge of your life. That's the end game you can aim for. When dealing with a narcissist, you must look at any situation you've been put in or any event that has happened. Look at it and see what your reactions are to it. Are those particular reactions warranted? How do they make you feel internally? Ascertain if you have a piece that contributed to the situation. Take accountability for whatever part you may have played, but lay down the rest, and don't be bullied, insulted, or allow guilt to make you pick it up again.

Things to Consider in Order to Break Free

1. Recognize if you're in a relationship with a narcissist and what responsibility in this relationship you need to take. What is keeping you here?
2. Are you even solely responsible for the success of the relationship?
3. Acknowledge some your behaviors, realizing you may be impacting multiple other relationships because of this one.
4. What steps can you take to stand up for yourself?

CHAPTER THREE

The Betrayal of Trust

Do not look for healing at the feet of those who broke you.
—Poet Rupi Kaur

W hich is worse? One incident of sexual abuse or a lifetime? I had never asked that question until I sat in a Twelve Step meeting thirty-five years ago. I heard the gut-wrenching stories of many who had endured years and sometimes decades of sexual abuse. It was easy for me to discount my childhood sexual abuse. After all, it only happened once. Yet, that one time messed with my head for almost my entire life until I reached the age of fifty-two.

It happened when I was in the third grade and had just changed into some play clothes after getting home from school. I chose my favorite outfit: a pair of blue shorts and a red and white checkered Western-style shirt fastened with white pearl snaps. I was anxious to get outside and bat the tetherball around the pole. Lost in my thoughts and not paying attention to my actions, I got hit in the head as the ball swung around the pole.

I was thinking about an adventure I had been on with my stepbrother Randy four days earlier. He didn't allow me to tag along with him and his friends very often. I liked it when he did. When we were alone, I thought we were a team, the two of us against our selfish, ridiculing, and violent parents–especially my dad. I could ignore the fact that his mom treated her precious boy as if he could do no wrong. Things were always my fault.

I trusted Randy, and I would do anything for him. I followed him anywhere he let me. Randy poked his head out the door, startling me and interrupting my daydream.

Wearing a big grin, he said, "Hey, do you want to come to my room and play a game with Mark and me?"

I ran toward him enthusiastically, swinging my arms back and forth, almost tripping on the way to the back door. He rolled his eyes at my eager clumsiness.

With curiosity, I asked, "What are we going to do?" *Maybe they want to play cards or build a fort with blankets?*

Randy ignored my question. Instead, he slipped inside the house, heading for the steps that led downstairs to his bedroom. Then he called behind him, "Are you coming?"

I hurried through the door, content. I was so grateful to be included in something with my brother. Feeling on top of the world, I replied, "I'm coming!" as I hurried down the steps. Randy and Mark were waiting in Randy's room, standing beside the bed. I could smell Randy's cheap cologne, which surprised me since he rarely wore any.

A weird feeling came over me. Something felt off, but I didn't quite know what.

Then my brother made the oddest request. "Take your clothes off and lie down on my bed." Mumbling, he added, "We want to try something."

I just stood there, not sure if I had heard him correctly. *Why do you want me to do that?* Randy repeated, speaking a little louder, "Take your clothes off and lie down on my bed."

I did not want to disappoint my brother, so I did as I was told. Slowly, I moved toward the bed, thinking, *it must be part of the game.*

I felt sick to my stomach, fumbling with my shoes and socks as I slowly removed each piece of clothing and laid down on my brother's bed and tried to cover myself with my trembling hands.

"We are putting a towel over your face, so you can't see anything," my brother explained with a threatening tone. "You better not tell anyone, or you'll be in big trouble."

While I lay there completely naked, blinded by the towel, my thoughts began to race. I was too afraid to remove the towel from my face for fear of what Randy would do. Sucking in my cheeks as if I could swallow my nervousness, my body stiffened when I felt a touch on my thigh. *Why is*

Randy touching me? Why is he doing this? This isn't a game I've ever played before.

I couldn't figure out what they were up to. But I did know it was not okay, whatever *it* was. I laid there frozen, petrified about letting them see my body, especially *down there*. My head was spinning. *What is going to happen?*

I don't remember exactly what happened next because I went somewhere else in my mind. I learned later I had dissociated because I was unable to stay in my body mentally. All I know is that when they finally stopped, I felt numb and scared to move. I did not know what to say or do. I continued to lay there with my face still hidden under the towel.

When I heard Randy's voice next, it sounded like he was leaving the room. "You better not even be thinking about telling anybody, *or you'll be sorry!*" he menaced.

The next thing I heard was the two boys laughing as they climbed the steps. My body started to shake with anger, and I cried uncontrollably. *How could Randy have done that? I don't understand.*

I was feeling vulnerable and exposed. I picked my clothes up off the floor to get dressed. My fingers didn't work. My eyes were filled with so many tears I prayed they would be gone when I made my way up the stairs and through the kitchen so I could hide in my room for the rest of the day.

I shut my door tightly behind me, convincing myself my brother could not be held responsible for what had happened. I thought even though it was Randy who had asked me to play and had made the threat, I rationalized it must have been Mark's idea.

I crawled into bed, shoes and all, pulling the covers over my head, and grabbed my little blue radio, putting it next to my ear as I wept until I fell asleep.

I dreamt I was on the playground at Glendale Elementary, and there, all my classmates gathered near the tricky bars watching me perform. My brown hair was long and pulled into a ponytail, held with a rubber band and a bright red ribbon. It slowly began pulling free with each spin. I heard someone count each time I went around. When I heard the count of fifty, I knew I had set the playground record. As I swung my body off to dismount, my hair came loose, and the ribbon was on the ground, but I didn't care. I stood there beaming when my teacher, Mrs. Rabbiger, threw her arms around my shoulders and declared, "Susan now holds the new playground record with fifty spins!" Everyone clapped as I soaked in all the praise.

It was late in the afternoon when I woke up, and I knew Mom would be home from work soon, but I stayed in my room as long as possible, not wanting to see my brother.

Nothing had been how I had believed it was. He didn't care about me. The bond I thought we had wasn't real. I was crushed. From then on, I avoided hanging around Randy, especially when he was together with Mark. For the first time in my life, I felt ashamed and labeled myself broken.

What I did know was that yes, I *couldn't* tell anybody, as if there was anyone I *could* even speak to. First, I blamed myself because I had allowed it to happen. And second, even if I did tell my parents, I was sure they wouldn't believe me. I knew this: nothing was going to happen to Randy. After all, he was Mom's cherished boy. Instead, I soothed myself in the privacy of my bedroom.

From that point forward, I came straight home after school to get there before Randy did, hiding in my room, where I took solace in having a snack. Food became my companion. My snack was usually a peanut butter and jelly sandwich. I used the back of a spoon to spread the creamy substance on the bread, taking an extra spoonful to eat on the side. I gradually added more to my plate, including pickles and potato chips. I was careful to hide any evidence of my after-school binges.

When I was almost eleven, I began noticing changes in my body. There was an abnormal secretion in my panties, and I was terrified. I believed to my core that it was because of what Randy and Mark had done to me.

To hide the evidence, my ten-year-old self came up with a solution to my situation. I folded layers of toilet paper to protect myself about my secret. I was afraid my mom would find out when she did the laundry. And *then* I would be in big trouble.

I did not understand that it was all part of the regular changes that a girl's body goes through when puberty hits. Nothing had been explained to me. My parents never talked to me about my body, let alone the impending physical changes. I knew that it was paramount to hide my secret from Mom.

Shortly after my eleventh birthday, my mom came into my room so we could have the "talk." She told me about menstruation and that she would get my sanitary pads when it was time. That's all she said before she walked out of my room, leaving me feeling dumbfounded and clueless. She had left out the part about what happens in puberty and the sex education part. Back then, it wasn't part of the school curriculum, so it was left up to the parents to educate their children.

I was consumed with fear daily, but I could only suffer in silence. There was no one I could talk to, not even my dear grandma. I wanted someone to put their arms around me and tell me everything was okay.

Anytime I thought about what had happened, the magnitude of brokenness and shame increased. Unable to escape the pain I was feeling inside, I turned toward food even more. It was comforting. I was still eating my way into a coma every day after school. Food became my protector, my best friend. It kept me from feeling any horrific feelings I didn't know how to handle.

When I started junior high school, I was happy to be out of elementary school but nervous about gym class. I dreaded having to undress in front of all the other girls in the locker room before we had to report to the gymnasium. How on earth was I going to be able to hide my secret? My solution was to dilly-dally on my way to the locker room after class ended. Therefore, I'd be the last one in the shower room and the last one back into the locker room to get dressed again. I still believed there was something very wrong with me.

In the '60s, girls were not allowed to wear pants to school. The worst part was that there wasn't a way to keep my toilet paper secure. I was highly fearful it would fall out at school. Then *everybody* would know. I would be laughed at and teased forever. After each class, I became exceedingly vigilant, going to the girl's bathroom to check myself and frequently making me late for my next class.

In eighth grade, one day in late November, the wind was blowing hard and making it frigidly cold. There were patches of ice on the pathways between the buildings at school from the snowstorm the day before. I was headed to do one of my in-between class checks in the bathroom. My legs burned as I power-walked as fast as I could. That's when I slipped and fell on the ice.

It was on that very day that my worst fears came to pass. My books and papers flew out of my arms like a spray of confetti, scattering all over the ground. I was mortified when I realized my wad of toilet paper had also slipped out. There it was, displayed on the sidewalk, visible for the world to see! As I scrambled to collect my stuff, I surveyed the area. I noticed there wasn't a soul around because the bell had already rung. I had dodged the bullet.

Throughout high school, I was awfulized by my abuse as the years passed. I convinced myself it was highly possible that I would not be able to have children. In the culture I was raised in, I was expected to marry and to have children soon after getting married. Compounding my misery was the realization I would need to reveal that shortcoming to any prospective beau. Because I believed I couldn't have children, everyone would find out about my secret. I was trapped in my own mind.

From Shame to Freedom

When I was twenty-nine, I drove to my dad's house, finally getting up the nerve to tell Dad about the abuse I had suffered in third grade at the hands of his stepson. His response wasn't different from what he had always done, although I prayed it would be better this time. As usual, he made it all about himself. "I did the best I could do!" he yelled defensively. Unsupported by my dad, I swallowed my feelings once again and left.

Still, this abuse ate at me in the dark recesses of my mind. It wasn't present in my everyday reality, but it still lurked in the shadows. I hadn't seen my brother for over seven years, and it had been more than three decades since my abuse. At age thirty-eight, I decided to write a letter to Randy. I needed to confront him about what he and Mark had done to me. I chose to write a letter rather than have an in-person unscripted conversation with him.

I didn't know what Randy's response would be, but I wanted him to know the magnitude of pain and misery he had caused. If it was written in black and white, he couldn't deny me the satisfaction of watching him read it in front of me. I was hoping Randy would say he was sorry. And at the very least, I wanted him to acknowledge what he had done.

I drove to Randy's house to place my letter in his hands. Mustering up all the courage I could, I knocked on the door. I nervously fidgeted with the zipper on my jacket while he read it. Afterward, he looked me straight in the eye. "We didn't do anything to you," he snarled. "I don't know what you're talking about!"

"Oh yes, you do," I retorted. "And I have lived with this catastrophic pain for over thirty years."

With a smirk on his face, he slammed the door, dismissing me.

On my drive home, I realized that even though I didn't get the results I had hoped for, I was proud of myself because I could finally say the words I had wanted-needed-to say for all those years.

After that incident, I began seeing a therapist to work on the issues of my abuse and the residual trauma from my childhood. We also worked through the residual issues stemming from my early relationships with people I was in a relationship with as an adult. I could make peace with myself, and I forgave Randy, but not for him, for me. It was so I could let the poison go for me. Forgiving him but certainly not forgetting what happened and not condoning it, I was able to let go of the shame and guilt, and it set me free!

Things I Learned

When working with women in the Utah State Prison, most of the participants chose to share they had suffered sexual, physical, emotional trauma as a child or young adult. It didn't mean it was the reason they ended up incarcerated, but it did have a significant effect on their self-esteem and, therefore, their ongoing choices. I have heard many women share that the only way they could endure an act of sexual abuse or sexual violence was to disassociate from their bodies. It gave them some sense of control. I now understand I had used dissociation as the defense mechanism so I could endure what was happening to me while I was lying on my stepbrother's bed so many years ago.

According to RAINN, the nation's largest anti-sexual violence organization, one American is sexually assaulted every sixty-eight seconds. And every nine minutes, that victim is a child.[2]

I learned it is important to have the courage to face your abuse, your shame, and your fears. The earlier you do this, the fewer years you have to carry that shame in the shadows. Like many women and men I work with, I did not "know better to do better." Also, please note that when you do face sexual abuse in any of its forms, it can sometimes feel like you are re-experiencing painful events in the present when you are thinking about it. This full-body response can indicate a somatic flashback, feeling as if it were happening right then. Getting help from a licensed therapist is essential if this is the case.

In taking back your power, own your voice. If you can bring justice, it is fair for you to do this. I had to recognize that even if Randy had apologized and admitted what he had done, at the end of the day, *the only one who could heal me was me.* This realization took years of talk therapy and many other techniques, which I will discuss in further chapters in this book.

I stayed in the mire and muck until I allowed myself to talk to someone, feel my feelings, and let them go. I needed to forgive others, but most importantly, myself. I did not know what I knew now. And while I may have been wounded at the hand of others, I am responsible for my healing, just as you are for yours. I have learned how to become my own hero.

Take the stand. Heal it. Become free. You hold the key to that freedom. This I know: you can too.

CHAPTER FOUR

Overcoming Labels to Create Your Destiny

We need to know our own identity before embracing our soul purpose.
—Madison Frederick

Y ou were given a name at birth, and along with the name comes a label—a daughter, son, granddaughter, etc. As we float through our lives, we put additional labels on ourselves, often based on the state of our self-esteem. It's the foundation for the narrative of the story you tell yourself. *Is* it important or even possible to change some labels or identifiers? No, not all of them. But the ones that don't suit you or support you? Oh, yes, it can be done!

There are different ways to use the word "identity." When applying for a loan, you are required to supply documentation proving you are who you say you are. Applying for employment requires proof that you can work in your country of origin or another country on special work visas. Belonging to a religious organization, a political party, or a non-profit corporation can also require an identifier.

What I am talking about in the context of identity in this chapter is how you identify or describe *yourself.* If you are someone who has experienced trauma-and most humans have or will at some point-it will likely originate from a negative experience, which in turn can easily create a negative belief about yourself, even as a way to keep yourself safe. Your brain wants to avoid that pain again, so as I shared in the last chapter, it may label you or the experience so that you don't find yourself in the same situation again, if possible. Unfortunately, it's not a failsafe and those negative labels and stories can stay with us long after the trauma.

In addition, people in our circles can make assumptions and judgments about us, usually based on their first impressions, where they often assign a label as a way to describe us. On my driver's license, my eye color will always be hazel, and I will always identify as right-handed. However, I have changed my name. What we are talking about are identifiers from trauma, such as "I am not good enough, I am not pretty enough, I'm not strong enough, I'm not brilliant enough. I am broken, and I'm not . . . enough."

I finally realized that the belief I was not good enough, which I carried as a self-imposed label for far too long, was something I *could* change just like I could change my name when I was old enough.

Bruce Hood, author of *The Self Illusion: Who Do You Think You Are?*, said, "Who we are is a story of our self —a constructed narrative that our brain creates."

True identity, on the other hand, is sometimes referred to as the authentic self. It's what happens when you get to the truth of who you truly are. When I chipped away all of the top layers or the facade of my life, my authentic self emerged. In letting go of those negative beliefs, my confidence in myself grew. I no longer resonated with most of the labels I had worn for decades.

Once I learned who I was and what I believed in, an amazing thing happened: I discovered my life's purpose. It didn't happen overnight; I needed to go through many phases to get there.

Becoming a Part of Something Bigger

My mom worked in the medical records department at the University of Utah Medical Center. The summer before I entered the ninth grade, she told me she had arranged for me to volunteer as a candy striper. I was to start the next day. I wondered if she had an ulterior motive and that was so she could keep an eye on me during the summer.

When I went to bed that night, however, I was so excited I couldn't sleep. My monkey brain spun a tale as big as an Oscar-winning movie. I envisioned myself working side by side with a handsome doctor, like the reigning teenage heartthrob, Richard Chamberlain, who played Dr. Kildare on the popular television program by the same name. As I finally drifted off to sleep, I decided it didn't matter if my stepmother had ulterior motives to keep track of me during the summer break. I now envisioned myself saving lives every day alongside Dr. Kildare.

When we pulled into the parking lot, I marveled at the wall of glass windows that looked like shimmering, solid ice. As the sun streaked through the windows, I noticed the tiny prisms framing each glass panel, creating rainbows. I could feel the warmth penetrate my entire body and a surge of overwhelming happiness. *A fresh new start.*

I thought I had hit the big time; I felt so grown up. I would be of service and out from underneath the cruelty I was shown at home. I thought my stepmother would be nicer to me when her coworkers were around. Upon entering the building, doctors and nurses strode confidently toward their assigned departments. Doctors were dressed in white monogrammed lab coats, and the nurses' shiny stethoscopes hung around their necks like fashion accessories. I could hardly contain myself. It *was* just like I had seen on Dr. Kildare!

When my stepmother took me to the volunteer director's office, Mrs. Green gave me my red- and white-striped pinafore. She informed me I was to report to the pediatric unit on the third floor. I would be reading stories to the children. I was nervous and excited at the same time. I made a pit stop in the gift shop to get myself a favorite candy bar to soothe my nerves. For years now, snacks were not only a reward but also my go-to when I needed to calm myself down. My first shift was all I had hoped for. I went home that afternoon as if floating on air.

The next day I was assigned to work in the gift shop. I loved being there and greeting the staff as they came in for their snacks throughout the day. I started to get to know some of them.

Quite often, these medical staff would discuss medical treatments or procedures with me. Even though I didn't understand most of what they were talking about, it all sounded intriguing, and I tried to absorb their knowledge. I fantasized I was in training to become a nurse–part of something greater and important, and I was making a difference in a small way.

During my break, I often ate lunch in the cafeteria with my stepmother.

One day two weeks after I started working there, I was waiting for her to finish something at her desk. My stepmother's friend, Irma, stood dead center of the doorway, blocking foot traffic in and out of the room. I didn't care too much for Irma; she constantly gossiped during any meal we shared together and was a real smartass. When I looked at her, I saw a gray-faced, sad woman who was very rough around the edges.

"I have a surprise for you," Irma announced that day, looking at me. "Come here."

Reluctantly, I walked over to her just as she proclaimed she had composed a little song and dance in honor of my name. "It's called 'the Susan Mae ditty,'" she said with laughter in her voice.

As I slowly walked across the room, all I could think about was how I had made it clear to my family that I hated to be called by my full name. I was born on my aunt's birthday, so we shared the same middle name, Mae. I hated my middle name with a purple passion.

Irma proceeded to do this little jig, kicking up her heels, reminding me of the Lucky Charms leprechaun as she sang. I won't dignify it by saying she had composed anything worth singing, but it certainly drew *everyone's* attention to her performance. About twenty people were laughing at this spectacle on display. My ears rang with pain from the sound of all the laughter. Everyone was looking at me.

I could have sworn I heard someone say, "What kind of a name is *Susan Mae?*" The question went through my mind. *Why couldn't my name have been Julie Ann, the name my birth mother Margaret had wanted to name me?*

Maybe I *didn't* hear anyone vocalize it, but the agony I felt went straight to my heart, ripping it apart. I reeled with horror and shame.

Choking back my tears long enough to make my escape before anything else was said, I bolted from the room and ran straight to the bathroom. Feeling sick to my stomach, I judged myself as worthless as always. Plus, I was hurt, furious, and felt betrayed.

I can't believe my mom would just stand there watching the performance, laughing and letting Irma do that to me! How could she? To make things worse, she didn't even bother to come look for me.

As I looked at my tear-streaked, twelve-year-old face in the mirror, my eyes were almost swollen completely shut. Muttering under my breath, I thought, *I hate my name, and now this!* I held my mother responsible for the whole debacle. Irma would not have known my middle name unless my mother had told her. *Gladys must have been making fun of my name with her friend all along.* Now I had even more of a reason to hate my name.

I made the decision that I would not be called Susan for one more minute. I was determined I would only answer to "Sue." This incident cemented my plan to change it legally to something I could love, and I needed to just endure my given name until I got old enough to do something about it.

Eating My Way through My Pain

After I was finally ready to leave the bathroom, I made my way to the gift shop for my afternoon shift. I felt safe working there by myself. I was grateful I would be able to lick my wounds in solitude.

The moment I stepped through the door, I spied all the candy bars displayed on several shelves and heard them calling my name. I spent the rest of that afternoon fueling my unrealized food addiction and numbing the pain I had experienced from my lunch break.

I ate my way into oblivion. In addition to candy bars, there were Hostess Ding Dongs, potato chips, and fruit pies. After eating all the junk food I had essentially stolen, shame consumed me; I began to feel sick from all the sugar I had just inhaled. When we got home, I skipped dinner and hid in my room.

At the end of the summer, I had volunteered well over two hundred hours as a candy striper. On the outside, I felt 90 percent proud of my work, but there was also remorse for eating all of the snack foods in the gift shop that day. Unfortunately, that day of binging on candy bars was not isolated.

The good news is this experience of working in a medical center gave me a sense of worthiness in service. It laid the foundation for my identity as a healthcare worker that spanned decades.

Creating a Label for Yourself Is a Way to Belong

When I started going to Twelve Step meetings at age thirty-four, the building we met in was an old church with two floors. The top floor was where the meetings were held. The bottom floor contained a snack bar with a dozen or so tables. People enjoyed nachos or hot dogs and soda after attending a meeting. It was commonly called "the meeting after the meeting" when we talked and smoked. Most of the people there participated in AA meetings, so I felt at the time that many alcoholics believed Al-Anon wasn't necessary. I was among the minority as an Al-Anon.

I started smoking as a way for me to feel I belonged, attempting to earn the privilege of being there with my friends who identified themselves as alcoholics. I took on a false identity as a smoker to fit in. I didn't enjoy smoking, but I did it anyway, similar to the things I didn't want to do with my stepbrother Randy so I could feel a part of his crowd.

It's not that there was anything wrong with belonging to a group. I started smoking to please others. Later in life, I realized I could make better choices to fit in, and I joined other groups and communities that were closer to my authentic self. I love that I can call myself a member of Sheroes United. It is an organization founded to empower women and help them overcome trauma by focusing on education and advocacy. Within the organization, I give back, sharing my wisdom and the tools I have learned with women incarcerated in the Utah State Prison and elsewhere. We hold classes that help these women to rid themselves of labels and find their own true identities.

One of the women was on her fifth incarceration when she signed up to attend our class. She shared with me that after being released for the fourth time, she had purposely violated her parole because she believed there was nowhere she belonged except in prison. She was only able to identify herself as an inmate. After taking the class, she began to think of herself so much differently that she let go of the label she once wore as a felon. It just would take some work for her to accomplish it in all of her habits and behaviors, but for her, it was also a fresh, new, and positive start in the right direction. She shared just how powerful it was.

You might have noticed I don't go by the name of Susan or even Sue anymore. In my adulthood, I finally changed my name to Madison. With my legal name change, I also could let go of the hurt child labeled incorrectly and hurtfully. I took back my power and claimed my own name.

The Stories You Tell Yourself

- Do you see yourself as a victim? Or do you see yourself as in control of your choices?
- Are you a person in chronic pain all of the time? Or do you choose for your body to be free from pain?
- Are you someone who is constantly distracted? Or someone who can stay focused?
- Are you one who struggles in every relationship? Or are you one who enjoys the delicate dance of relationships, learning and growing alongside your friendships and partnerships?

In the book written by James Clear, *Atomic Habits: An Easy & Proven Way to Build Good Habits & Break Bad Ones*,[3] Clear teaches the concept of "habit stacking" to change your identity.

I wanted to change the habit of having a snack every afternoon. I had started comforting myself at four o'clock from the age of ten after my sexual abuse. It had been a struggle for me to manage my weight for many decades, and I believe my snacking was a good place to begin to put into play Clear's concept.

I realized I needed to be proactive in my approach. Following Clear's method of habit stacking, the first layer was to set the alarm on my phone at three-thirty, reminding me I needed to be anywhere but in the kitchen. The second thing I added or stacked upon the first habit was to take action when my alarm went off. I learned to keep myself busy by putting something in my hands, either reading or doing craft projects. Sometimes I would turn on the music and dance. Those steps have completely replaced my habit of having a snack at four o'clock. Over time, I built a healthy habit of staying out of the kitchen in the afternoon, filling myself with greater, more positive things. For additional help in becoming aware of the lables you have taken on, please go to www.madisonfredrick.com to download a worksheet that can assist you with this process.

Ikigai: A Japanese Philosophy to Claim Your Purpose

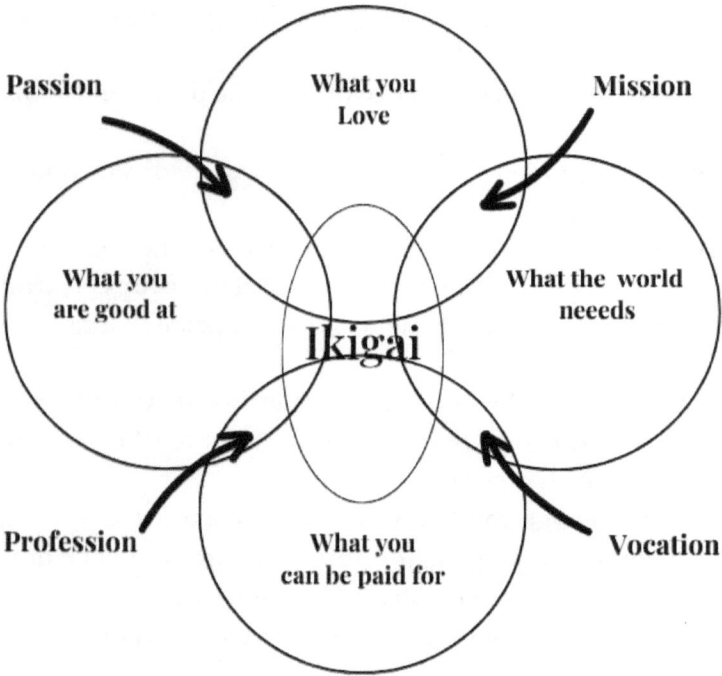

Ikigai is a Japanese word and philosophy that means "your reason for breathing," or passionately living your life purpose. There are four circles or quadrants overlapping one another that create your ikigai. They are Passion, Mission, Vocation, and Profession, all of which can motivate you to get up in the morning. It's important that you strive to live on target, meaning that you hit all four quadrants together. Represented in the very center is your ikigai, a place of knowing your life's purpose and enjoying your bliss.[4]

How Do You Discover What Your Ikigai Is?

It's important to ask yourself the following:

1. What do you love?
2. What are you good at?
3. What does the world need?
4. What can you be paid for?

After I got engaged, I focused on being happily married and having a family. I believed it was my calling, or life purpose, just like so many other young women in my culture. I abandoned my desire to go to nursing school, telling myself I was destined to be a homemaker. I was playing the part. I love my children, but I wanted more out of life than being a wife and mother–especially after my marriage to my first husband, Ron, fell apart. I was floating aimlessly, just like cottonwood tree seeds blowing in the wind, looking for a place to land to create new growth. I knew something was missing, but I didn't know what until I got healthier and started to thrive.

Sticking my big toe in the waters of the medical field after my divorce, I trained as a Recreational Therapist Technician. From that time on, I made a career in helping people with disabilities. The passion I have felt for helping people continues to float my boat.

It wasn't until I learned the ikigai philosophy, however, that I fully understood the importance of knowing precisely what my life's purpose was. Opportunities expanded beyond recreational therapy to include solutions for people–not just physical challenges but mental challenges that keep people stuck.

Discerning what your life mission is can bring you happiness and joy in your daily life, especially if there is that balance in all four quadrants. It means continuous steam in your engine to do powerful things in the world upon the winds of your passion. You must first find what you are passionate about and then look for a way to implement a method in your life.

A powerful example of this is Scott Harrison, who, in 2006, founded Charity Water and found his passion for ending the water crisis around the world. As of the writing of this book, Charity Water has funded 91,414 wells and water projects in twenty-nine countries. Scott is continuing to live his dream, realizing his passion for service and being able to do it well and fund his passion all along the way.

Your ikigai will be more fully discovered and fleshed out as you figure out what you love, and what you're good at (or are passionate enough that you are willing to become better at your skillsets) to do more of what you love. You will know if the vocation you are considering will give you financial rewards that will sustain your lifestyle because not only is it what the world needs, but you'll be rewarded financially for doing it. Just like anything in life, you must go after it and be willing to fail while learning so that, just like Scott, you can persevere and succeed.

> *The equation for purpose is G+P+V=P.*
> *(gifts + passions + values = purpose).*
> *—Richard Leider*

CHAPTER FIVE

What Happened to My Fairytale?

*It's not necessary to play a part in someone else's bad
behavior just to feel secure in a relationship.*
—*Madison Frederick*

There is a difference between helping someone and enabling someone. Do you know the definition of enabling? Enabling generally describes someone who allows destructive behavior to continue, such as using illegal substances. Sometimes this includes supporting such unhealthy things as free rent for too long or paying for multiple stints in a treatment center for substance abuse.

As humans, it can be difficult to tell if you are enabling someone or being kind. This especially was true early in my life and in my early relationships. So how do you know?

These are some signs and characteristics of an enabler:

1. Do you ignore or tolerate problematic behavior like addiction, anger, or abuse?
2. Do you provide financial assistance or buy things for someone when they should take care of it themselves?
3. Are you making excuses for someone's behavior towards yourself and others?
4. Do you take responsibility for more than your share of a workload?
5. Do you make light of a situation, brushing it off as no big deal?
6. Do you deny there is a problem?
7. Do you sacrifice your own needs over the needs of others?

Empowerment is when you let someone take responsibility for

themselves. Regardless of doubts you may have that it will be done correctly, do not assume you could do it better and take on the responsibility yourself. Let them make mistakes. It is the way they learn and grow.

Was It Real Love?

I got to know my future mother-in-law when we worked together in a convalescent center. I was just seventeen years old. During our break time, she told me about her son, who was in the navy and stationed on an aircraft carrier homeported in Norfolk, Virginia. She encouraged me to write him a letter. I "met" Ron during my senior year of high school via the United States Post Office.

In the beginning, my reason for writing him was to do my part in the Vietnam War effort, just like the cultural icon Rosy the Riveter from WW II, whom I had learned about in my history class.

Three months after receiving his first letter, he came to Salt Lake on a weeks-long leave.

I nervously rode to the airport with his family (most of them I had never met) to greet him. When I saw him just beyond the gate, I was taken aback by how handsome he looked in his dress blues uniform. As he walked closer, I saw his deep blue eyes smiling joyfully. He stood five feet, seven inches tall with medium brown hair in a military-style cut.

Ron swept me off of my feet. For the week, we spent as much time together as we could between my work schedules. It was a whirlwind romance that concluded with my left hand being adorned with a diamond nestled in a yellow-gold setting. Although I had always preferred white gold or silver, I didn't want to say anything, partly because I didn't want to hurt his feelings and partly because I didn't want to bother him with having to go through the hassle of exchanging it. I didn't want to make waves or inconvenience my fiancé.

That was the beginning of what would be my pattern of not speaking my mind throughout my marriage. I was still discounting myself in my mind. I thought I wasn't worth inconveniencing anyone, as I had done most of my life. I swallowed my disappointment. I told myself I was lucky because there weren't many girls at school who were already engaged and had a destination waiting for them after graduation.

When Ron returned to Virginia, I took extra shifts to save money for our wedding. He had been gone for five months when he received orders to report to the Naval Air Station in Lemoore, California, in September. He wanted to move there as a brand-new couple, even though there wasn't much time to plan a wedding. We decided we would marry within the next month and a half of him reporting for his next duty station. I was eighteen; he was twenty-two. Ron and I had a small wedding ceremony with about seventy-five people on the guest list.

The truth was we didn't know each other when we got married. Looking back on it, I think I was more excited about moving away from my parents than the actual wedding itself. I did know I was determined to have a completely different marriage than what was modeled for me by my parents. I never witnessed them working together on anything. I wanted a different marriage than what my parents modeled. I noticed their communication style or lack thereof while growing up. I didn't witness my parents discussing anything about anything.

When I married, I envisioned working with my husband as a team. I was under the impression that Ron and I were on the same page regarding that strategy. We talked about how we had seen our parents *not* talk about things. I trusted everything Ron told me, including when he shared his desire to work together and make decisions as a couple. I was relieved we had agreed.

Neither of us knew how to set any personal goals in life, let alone as a couple. Although we were flying by the seat of our pants, I was optimistic it would be a great marriage. The only problem was that I had no idea what that looked like.

Two months after we tied the knot, Ron had seen an autumn bronze 1969 Chevrolet Chevy SS on a car lot before we made our move. Ron wanted us to have a bigger car because he thought my car was too small. He mentioned he had always dreamt of owning a sports car. He suggested we trade in my Volkswagen and buy the Chevy because it would be better for "us." Ron justified it by saying if something broke on my bug, he wouldn't know how to fix it, unlike an American-made car.

I loved my little gray bug, dents and all. It had been my ticket to freedom from the trauma and stress I had been experiencing at home with my dad and mom daily. I wasn't crazy about giving up my car, especially when I sat behind the steering wheel of the new car; it felt like I was driving a boat. The front seat was big enough to lie down and take a nap. Swallowing my feelings of disappointment, I gave in–just as I was so accustomed to doing my entire life. With deep regret, I sacrificed my car for my and Ron's marriage. After all, it was my contribution to our "team."

When we arrived in California, I was committed to becoming the very best wife I could be. Upon pulling into the city of Hanford, literally the first exit off the highway, we drove straight into the parking lot of the first apartment complex we had seen a vacancy notice. I wanted to look at other places, but Ron insisted we move in there. He told me he was too tired from driving for the last twelve hours.

Acting as the supportive wife, I gave in once more. We paid the deposit and the first month's rent. That was how we navigated our finances and our lives, with Ron getting his way and jumping in before we looked. We made many purchases based on what Ron wanted. We bought over a dozen cars during the seventeen years we were married. It was always Ron's choice.

Our first apartment came completely furnished and felt nice and cozy. The ten-unit complex housed mostly military couples of lower-ranking men who didn't qualify for base housing. Our neighbors, Pam and Todd, often invited us to play cards. I enjoyed Pam's company while the guys drank beer and discussed the world's ways. It was my first taste of living in a military community. I loved being a navy wife. The camaraderie I felt with military people was like the family I never had.

I had a rough start during my attempt at cooking corn on the cob, not realizing I needed to take the husk off first. I knew I needed help. With *Betty Crocker's Dinner For Two Cookbook,* I taught myself how to cook. I was content with fulfilling the role of a housewife. I liked to have dinner ready when Ron returned home from work, like June Cleaver on the *Leave It to Beaver* television program. Although I didn't own a pearl necklace like the one June wore, I did make myself an apron with bright red bunches of cherries nestled on a white background. It had two big pockets trimmed with red ruffles.

Our relationship blossomed. Ron and I even had pet names for each other. He was Babycakes, and I was Pumpkin. I thought I had come into my own and I belonged. Doing the shopping, making dinner, and even being responsible for our laundry gave me confidence; I felt like an adult.

I loved to tease Ron. Once I sewed the fly of his underwear shut as a practical joke. I imagined him calling me from work and we would have a good laugh. He didn't call, but as soon as he walked through the door of our tiny apartment and saw the mischievous look on my face, he realized I had been up to no good. "What's wrong, Babycakes?" I giggled as I wrapped my arms around him.

"It was you!" he exclaimed with glee in his eye and a smile in his voice. "I thought I had my underwear on backward all day!"

Ron swooped me up in his arms and carried me to the bedroom. Like Rhett Butler from *Gone with the Wind* had carried Scarlett O'Hara up the stairs to make passionate love, Ron was my Rhett. I was deliriously happy with our love relationship.

From the very beginning of our marriage, I was always trying to "fix Ron" in the guise of helping. I thought I was supporting my husband. I felt he needed my help with things when he probably didn't.

I justified doing Ron's GED certificate exams via the post office to ease his burden. The outcome of my "helping" Ron was my first step on my way to my learned behavior called enabling. Doing so, I cut the legs out from underneath him by doing things *for* him. It was another layer I developed on my way, leading to many problems in all of my relationships.

My husband and I didn't fight very often for the first few months, but when we did, like many couples, it was usually about money. I was in charge of managing our household budget and developed the habit of robbing Peter to pay Paul when it came time to pay the bills, making sure there were beer and cigarettes in the house. Money was always tight.

One of the ways I did this was to write up a grocery list before I went shopping. I would take the receipt from the prior payday's shopping and use it as a template. Before I went, I calculated how much the groceries would cost, as close to the penny as possible. I clipped coupons and planned my meals around them. It would determine what I could buy for the next two weeks based on the cost of each item needed after looking at the previous grocery receipts.

Carefully, I always kept in mind the amount of money I needed to purchase cigarettes and beer for the next two weeks. It made me a bit nervous, not knowing if I would have enough cash when I got in the check-out line. I usually did pretty good, but one time, I was thirty-eight cents short; I had to leave the store without peanut butter.

Even with my careful planning, usually four or five days before the next payday, Ron would be out of beer and cigarettes. It became a source of stress for me. I knew smoking was an addiction, so for Ron, not having cigarettes would be very difficult, especially when he was at work. I fretted about it. Almost all his coworkers smoked, yet Ron didn't like to bum cigarettes from anyone.

Since he usually ran out of beer, too, before the next shopping trip, I started to hide an extra six-pack and a pack of cigarettes in what I had come to know as the beer closet, thinking it would slow Ron's consumption when he was almost out. Hiding additional supplies, I thought, was the only way I could think of to manage the situation. Unfortunately, he soon got wise to that tactic and quickly blew through the extra as well.

I wanted to protect myself from Ron's anger when he ran out of his vices. When he didn't have his supplies, especially his beer, he verbally took it out on me. Ron would thrash me with his words, sometimes leaving the room and slamming the door behind himself. I didn't realize it at the time, but his sudden harshness was his withdrawal from nicotine and alcohol.

When Ron and I lived in California for about a year, Ron's squadron prepared for an extended deployment overseas. He also had to go on several shorter deployments leading up to the long one. One of those he was scheduled to go to Fallon, Nevada, so the pilots could practice their touch-and-go landings. He would be gone for three weeks.

We both agreed I should find work to earn extra money. I took a job in a nursing home as a nursing assistant, a vocation I already knew and was good at.

I loved my new job and was scheduled to work the day Ron was to return home. We never knew in advance what time of day the squadron would be coming back. Surely, he would arrive long before my shift started. But I soon got a call from one of the other wives telling me they'd be home much later than we had been informed earlier that morning.

I calculated that I had enough time to pick up Ron and take him home before my shift started. As we walked to the car, I told him we needed to hurry because I didn't want to be late for work.

Ron had assumed I would take the day off, and he became very angry with me when he found out that wasn't the case. He wanted me to call in sick. I refused, telling him they would be short-staffed if I did. He then took it even further, demanding I just quit.

I seethed through clenched teeth, "If you want me to quit, I will put in my two-week notice *when* I show up for my shift today."

"No, I want you to quit right now!" he ordered. "And if you don't call them, I will call them and quit for you."

Never in a million years did I think he would follow through. I stood there dumbfounded as he dialed the number. I was embarrassed as I listened to his side of the conversation, even though the person on the other side of the line couldn't see me. I felt my face flush, thinking, *How can I ever face someone in the front office when I pick up my last check?*

I was so distraught I blubbered through my tears as I hurried into the bathroom, shutting and locking the door behind me. *How could he do that to me?* I fumed inside. I sat on the toilet seat, held my face in my shaking hands, and sobbed.

After about half an hour of trying to convince me to come out, speaking through the locked door and changing tactics, he finally said, "But Pumpkin, I missed you. Why don't we get something to eat? Can I take you to McDonald's for dinner?"

Oh, he's pulling out the sucker punches now. He knew I liked Big Macs, fries, and a strawberry sundae, and food was always a way to comfort me.

What I Learned

I enabled Ron by doing the assignments for his GED because he told me he couldn't do them himself. I could have encouraged him instead of completing them myself, so he'd been successful.

I juggled money so I could buy the extra beer and cigarettes, instead of letting him do without, or figure it out himself. Obviously, my behavior of hiding stashes of beer and cigarettes to manage his anger and addiction was classic enabling behavior instead of empowering him to take responsibility. Plus, it never ended with a good outcome when I did things like that; it always backfired.

Things to Consider

- What is your understanding about enabling now?
- How is that different from supporting or helping?
- How can you turn around any of these enabling characteristics you may have?
- In what ways can you empower someone? Or how can you empower yourself?
- Where can you let someone feel the natural cause-and-effect consequences of their action?
- Is there a fine line between giving someone a helping hand and enabling them? After reading this chapter, can you count the number of times you have enabled someone?

Becoming aware of your behavior and setting boundaries *will* set you free. This not only frees up your time but also declutters your mind so you can focus on taking care of yourself.

CHAPTER SIX

True Confessions from Hong Kong

If you accept a limiting belief, then it will become a truth for you.
—Louise Hay

W hy would I stay in a broken marriage for so many years? I didn't believe in myself and didn't think I had any options for anything better. They were limiting beliefs I had about myself or situations. I believed I wasn't good, smart, or deserving of love, and my emotions drove my bus for over three decades and affected my choices. Through the years, I developed a plethora of limiting beliefs that held me back. It was only after I knew better that I did do better.

Are there places in your life where you are feeling stuck? Devalued? Unworthy of better?

Ron and I had been married for eight months when I got pregnant with our first child, a daughter. After hearing my test results, I walked out of the ob-gyn clinic feeling light in my body like a cloud floating up to the heavens. Although I was a little nervous, I was also very excited to start our little family.

What kind of mother will I be? I wondered. The way motherhood was modeled for me wasn't pretty. First came my birth mother, Margaret, who left us when I was three, then came my stepmom. Neither of them was the best or healthiest example.

My happy thoughts dampened on my drive home from the doctor's office. How on earth would I be able to pull *any* money from the household budget for the expenses of a new child? Not only for decorating the baby's room, but how could we afford all the equipment we would need?

I was still irritated that my husband had called the nursing home, telling them I had quit. He had severely cut our income, and our financial obligations hadn't diminished but grown. Plus, I had wanted to work because Ron would be departing on a long deployment for eight or nine months, and I would be alone. The thought of spending all those hours by myself haunted me.

In preparation for the lengthy deployment, Ron set up an allotment, or a portion of his paycheck, to be sent to me automatically each month. He would keep almost a third of each check for himself for "spending money." I was flabbergasted when he told me how much I would receive each month. How was I supposed to survive on six hundred dollars a month?

I asked him, "Why do you need to keep so much of your paycheck?"

"What? Don't you think I deserve to have a cold one when we get into port, and I finally have real time off?" he retorted with an attitude. "Besides, I'll send you a money order with any leftovers I don't spend!"

"Well, how do you think I'm going to be able to handle all the bills then?" I fired back. I knew it would be a long shot if any leftovers were sent back home to me in a timely manner for the bills to be paid. I had been told by some of the seasoned wives that the mail was not reliable once they left the States. "We're already struggling, especially with you making me quit my job!"

With a smirk on his face, he answered, "Oh, you'll figure it out."

Seventeen days before Ron was to leave on deployment, my contractions started. The delivery was more complicated than it should have been. I learned later from the delivery nurse that the doctor on duty was an underqualified pediatrician and had only seen a baby delivered in med school. He wanted to do the delivery to have his first experience delivering a baby and didn't want to call my obstetrician to come back into the hospital.

An episiotomy wasn't done, so I tore crookedly, preventing the doctor from adequately suturing the tear together. Then, I hemorrhaged to the point that they had to give me a transfusion. When my obstetrician was finally called in, to my relief, it took him almost an hour to repair all the damage. I was given a high dose of pain medication when I was discharged three days later, but I could hardly walk without being in a lot of pain.

My husband left for his deployment when our daughter was thirteen days old. The first port Ron's aircraft carrier pulled in to take on supplies was Manila in the Philippines. When he was able to call collect a couple of days later, we had a lengthy conversation about Ron *not* calling collect because of the expense.

After he'd been gone for an additional month, I was excited when they were scheduled to pull into Hong Kong any day. I spent that Friday morning playing with my baby. After I fed and rocked her to sleep, I put her in the crib for a nap. Just as I was coming out of her room, the phone rang. I was perturbed when I heard the operator ask if I would accept a *collect call* from Ronald Granger *again*.

I made a mental note, exasperated. *Great! Yet another huge phone bill I don't know how I'm going to pay.*

The first thing my husband said was, "I need to tell you something, Pumpkin. I feel so guilty I can't live with myself anymore." My heart surged up into my throat while he paused and added, "I just love you so much, and I need to tell you what I did because I can't live with myself any longer."

Did he borrow money he knows we don't have? I know he already spent every dime he had back in Manila. That behavior wouldn't surprise me.

That's when my husband proceeded to tell me he had gone home with a prostitute the last night they were in the Philippines . . . two months earlier. He didn't call her a prostitute; he called her a barmaid.

What's the difference? I thought. My husband stepped out on me–and paid for it with money we did not have in the first place. The money was the least of my shattered heart, however.

"I'm so sorry; I just couldn't help myself," he admitted. "I slipped. You didn't give me any before I left."

I sat there, dumbstruck, as if in a fog. *Did I just hear him say this is my fault?* My knees buckled and I sank into the couch. I wasn't prepared for what he said next.

Almost unconcerned, he added, "I had an idea of how we can spice up our lovemaking when I get home. One of the guys in the squadron told me about a book I think will improve our lovemaking. I went to the PX and picked up a copy. I mailed it to you so you can read it before I get back."

Are you kidding me? It wasn't lost on me that he had not bought one for himself so he could also read it. Barely able to breathe, I bumbled through my tears. I nearly choked on my words until they all came gushing out: "Just how in the hell can you blame *me* for you having a slip?" I screamed. "You *know* I was torn and still on heavy pain medication when you left."

In my mind, I wanted to add, *Our daughter was only thirteen days old when you deployed, asshole! Don't you remember? How dare you insinuate it's my fault we couldn't make love so soon after her birth–especially when the doctor said no?*

Ron persisted; his tone now defensive. "If I had been able to get any before I left, I never would have gone home with the barmaid!"

Ron, in essence, believed he had a legitimate excuse. And now that he had confessed, we could simply sweep it all under the carpet and move on. The rest of what he said was a big blur. I could tell he was drunk by how he rambled on and on. I tuned him out while he continued to justify himself. I mentally put my fingers in my ears and chanted silently to myself, *La la la la la la,* so I could drown out the hurtful words. What he said was so painful. It was unbelievable and too challenging for me to comprehend.

After we hung up, I assessed our love life quickly. I began questioning everything: my skills in the bedroom, my sexuality, not to mention my self-worth. I asked myself, *How did I get it all wrong? I thought we had a great sexual relationship! We were playful and caring for each other, and there was a lot of tenderness.*

Now what? I can't divorce Ron. I don't have any college education. And I have a child now. How can I support the two of us? When we got married, I was all in, believing Ron was as dedicated to our marriage as I was.

I wondered if I had been delusional about my marriage from the very beginning. Maybe it *was* my fault. Perhaps Ron hadn't been as satisfied as I had thought. I felt like a complete failure. Growing up, my parents never thought I was good enough, and now I believed it to be true: *I must not be sexy enough. Or good enough, as a wife or a woman, or even as a human being.* Those beliefs, labels, and many more were things I carried for decades that I believed were all true.

I had a choice to make. Did I choose to file for a divorce? Or did I suck it up and accept the accusation that I had failed my husband and, therefore, my marriage? I had no power. I had no choice, I thought. So, I settled for a man who drank too much, smoked too much, and was already unfaithful to me in the first eighteen months into our marriage. I felt so powerless; I simply resolved to make the best of it.

Having lived with my grandparents for many of my formative years, I saw firsthand how going to church had positively impacted our lives. I considered finding our local meeting place.

We were members of the Church of Jesus Christ of Latter-day Saints. While living with my grandparents, I was surrounded by families who read scripture, prayed together, and attended activities at the church building throughout the week. As an adult, I longed for that connection inside a religious community I once had. I thought it would "fix" things. As a member of the church, it was frowned upon if you smoked or drank. Therefore, if Ron quit using those things in addition to our happier family, it would be like killing two birds with one stone. Our marriage would be saved, and I would have God in my life. Sadly, I didn't follow through at that time.

When the phone bill arrived after his true confessions collect call about three weeks later, it was over four hundred dollars. In 1971, that was a massive amount of money. (At the time of this writing, that would be about $2,983!) I was beside myself. I didn't know how on earth I would come up with that kind of money. I thought about asking to borrow money from my dad, but I was far too ashamed to ask.

A week later, a friend mentioned she knew of someone who had gone to a tomato field and worked on the harvesting trucks. She told me that if I just showed up, and if there was room on a truck, I could just get on. The shift started at ten p.m. and ended at six in the morning.

It wasn't typical or expected that a non-Hispanic person would be out in the fields working alongside the migrant farmworkers. I was so desperate for money I decided to give it a try. I drove to the field and got on one of the work trucks in the middle of the field. We were out in the middle of nowhere; it was pitch black except for the lights we worked by on the inside of the machine. I felt intimidated, yet I was on a mission.

When the foreman came to check the number of workers on our machine, he said there were too many of us, and someone had to leave. Even though I was scared shitless, knees knocking, I was determined to stand my ground and work. I had a looming phone bill to pay, and I needed to take care of it, or the phone would be shut off.

I held my breath and prayed I wouldn't get sent home. I put my head down, didn't say a word, and just played stupid, acting like I had been there before. Out of the corner of my eye, I couldn't help but see the other workers were pointing at me, motioning with their heads for me to get off. Out of desperation, I held my ground.

I was petrified, and my imagination roamed all over the place. I hadn't told my friend I would try and work that night; the babysitter didn't know exactly where I was, except in some field. What if I got stabbed and dumped in the middle of nowhere? Maybe I'd become a victim of an unsolved murder. What would happen to my daughter if something happened to me?

What on earth was I thinking?

Luckily, the foreman decided to let it slide, so I was safe. With a sigh of relief, I waited for the belt to begin moving. As the tomatoes rolled by in front of me, it was my job to pull the rotten ones off. The swamp water smell of the fruit was almost unbearable. I hadn't brought any gloves, so my hands were filthy and sticky from the juice. I had to push my hair out of my face many times during the night. Juicy chunks of rotten tomatoes adorned my hair and felt like an application of L'Oréal mousse. No wonder the other workers wore bandanas.

When the shift ended, we all got off the machines and stood in line to get our pay. Out of the corner of my eye, I saw a short man with greasy hair hanging in his eyes stalking towards me with an angry gait. Putting his face so close to me, I could smell his rotting teeth. He threatened me in broken English to never to come back because I didn't belong.

I took a step back, keeping my eyes down. I grabbed my cash and ran to my car. I could hear my heartbeat pounding in my ears as I hurried. I locked the door and then sped away, not looking back. I was grateful I had earned money, but the work was so dangerous for me to be there.

I knew I couldn't go back. With the money I earned that night and juggling some other bills, I was able to take care of the phone bill.

When Ron returned home from the deployment, things were pretty strained. It was easier not to think about how I had been betrayed. I had been taught that I was to support my man no matter what, just like in the Patsy Cline song, *Stand by Your Man*. I pretended I was okay, but it was a lie. It would *never* be the same, nor would our marriage; things were unrepairable, but I soldiered on.

I did not trust anything Ron said. He was a liar and a very selfish manipulator, just like my dad. Looking back, I see that it was the beginning of everything coming unraveled. Even though I did continue to try to please my husband, I needed to stay because of my duty as a wife and mother.

In 1977, Ron received orders to report to Whidbey Island in Washington state. I hoped things would be different, especially since I was pregnant with our son. I suggested that going to church and having a Christian influence in our house would be good for our family. Ron agreed and we became members of the Catholic church. Ron liked the idea because there were no restrictions on smoking or drinking. The three of us were baptized. Ron was deployed for eight months. Upon returning home, our son, who was three months old, was also baptized.

The parish we belonged to offered a weekend couples retreat called Marriage Encounter. It was designed to teach a style of communication to strengthen marriages. On day two of the retreat, Ron walked out of the group meeting because he wanted to go home. It was another disappointment for me on a long list.

But for the next nine years, I continued to lie to myself, thinking there was hope things would get better, that *Ron* would get better. I was doing what was best for my family, I thought. I continued to try and fix everything.

Every argument I had with Ron resulted in me having a lump in my throat, choking back the words, "I want a divorce." I thought, *if we just talked things through, it'll all be okay. I will be able to figure out what I need to do to fix this, and I won't have to leave.*

In 1980, Ron received orders to Ewa Beach in Hawaii. Going to mass as a family was discontinued because Ron didn't like the priest. Again, I went along, trying to keep the peace. Continuing to drink a lot, he began to have blackouts. At least twice a week, he wouldn't remember things he'd said or some of the things he had agreed to do, and he claimed things were never discussed.

In May of 1985, we moved back to Utah and bought a house. Ron would be retiring from the navy and would be spending his last three years stationed aboard an aircraft carrier in California. We wanted to get established in Salt Lake before he retired. I told myself that once Ron retired and moved away from his drinking buddies, it would improve. But it didn't get any better.

We had a major argument about his drinking, and I told him I had gone to a lawyer and was filing for a legal separation, a precursor to a divorce. He swore to me once more he would quit drinking and offered to start going to the LDS church with me. Next, he promised to take me through the temple because he said he wanted to be married for time and eternity. This was a sacred process for members of our church, and he knew it pulled at my heartstrings.

Four months into his retired life, Ron hadn't fulfilled his promise to quit drinking and become an active member in the church. I simply had my "'nuffs"; I didn't believe the lies anymore about my worth and what I had to put up with, and I told Ron to leave. I began the process for a full divorce the following week. I still felt scared and nervous about what I would do; I fell into my old mind trap, believing I wasn't good enough to pull it off.

My dad quickly weighed in with his opinion. He told me I would never make it without a husband. But with the support and encouragement of my friends and a family member who believed in me, I permitted myself to return to school. I became a Recreational Therapist Technician and proudly bought my car. Slowly but surely, I chose to break free from the shackles placed on my life and soul and move forward in my life. It did not come in one day, but I learned I could break free from old, unhealthy, and untrue fixed beliefs. I believe if I can do that, so can you!

What I've Learned

A belief is a thought or opinion that we take to be the absolute truth, i.e., one make of car is better than another, or a sports team is the best no matter what number they are in the standings or reviews. Some beliefs can be called limiting beliefs. Here are some examples: *I'm not good enough, intelligent enough, pretty enough, handsome enough, rich enough, or educated enough.*

Growing up in a household where an organized religion overshadowed my whole life, I was taught to believe what "proper" behavior and attitude looked like to become labeled as a good mother. I believed men *always* had the final say, and I planned to follow my husband's lead when I got married, no matter what—even looking away when my husband's behavior was less than stellar. It was expected that I have children, and it was also my job to do the cooking and cleaning without question or complaint.

Although I loved and adored being a mother, my belief in myself was never very high. I stayed in my marriage as long as I did because of my belief that I was not good enough for anything or anyone else if I divorced. I didn't earn a degree in college, so I felt less than. I believed I was not thin or attractive enough to find anyone else. And I simply didn't think I could provide for my children.

Fixed beliefs can keep us stuck, settling for less, remaining unhappy, and spiraling into depression. It is a belief I considered to be the absolute truth–even though there was absolutely no proof it was so! Changing the ones we inherited from our families can feel like we would be going against the beliefs and/or traditions of the people we love. However, it is possible to overcome them, expand what is possible in our minds and hearts, take a stand for ourselves, and reach out for a better life! When we do this, we are also good examples to our friends and family who may be similarly stuck in old beliefs.

Powerful Steps To Consider

1. Identify and write down any negative thoughts you have about yourself and your life.
2. Where did each belief originate?
   - Is it based on generations of family beliefs and traditions?
   - Or, perhaps, was it something you were told during your childhood or as an adult?
3. What is the evidence that the belief was somehow valid?
4. Recognize it is just a belief and is not the truth.
5. Make a list of all the negative things you believe about yourself.
6. Looking at the entire list, rate them in order of importance.
7. Choose the top three to five beliefs and create a positive affirmation regarding each of them.
   Example:
   "I can't do anything right" becomes "I can do things the right way."
   "I'll never make enough money" can become "I always have more than enough money."
8. Preferably, while looking in a mirror, recite them daily.

You can go back and repeat the process with any remaining beliefs you wrote down.

You can enhance your affirmations by adding tools like meditation or dabbing essential oils, as you say them, to stimulate the brain into acting differently. (See my list of some of the oils I used in the back of the book.) For example, I used frankincense, the oil of truth, to better understand the truth about myself. Wild orange, the oil of abundance, championed me to discover my self-worth, and peppermint helped me to rise beyond my limiting beliefs.

Taking these steps enhanced my fortitude and emotional strength to move forward. I encourage you to take your own powerful steps and dance towards a new perspective on your own beliefs and what is now possible for you!

CHAPTER SEVEN

Head Games on Steroids

'You misunderstood what I meant,' he said.
'You misunderstand who I am,' she finally said.
—Madison Frederick

O ne of the statements my dad always used was, "You misunder-stood what I meant." When I heard this, I thought to myself, *Maybe I am delusional; perhaps he didn't mean it the way it sounded.* My dad used manipulation as part of his narcissistic behavior. I was not the only, first, or the last one victimized by his words, but they had a profound effect on me from a very young age. First off, I was not supposed to feel. He told me I was too sensitive and to quit wearing my feelings on my sleeves.

I began to believe him. For decades, I believed countless other state-ments too. Narcissism and behavior, often called "gaslighting," tend to go hand in hand in relationships. Because you've already been intro-duced to narcissism, I would like to share with you how gaslighting can play heavily in that process of control.

Merriam-Webster Definition of Gaslighting:

Gaslighting: Psychological manipulation of a person, usually over an extended period of time, causes the victim to question the validity of their thoughts, perception of reality, or memories, and typically leads to confu-sion, loss of confidence, and self-esteem, the uncertainty of one's emotional or mental stability, and a dependency on the perpetrator.

Gaslight is the name of a play from the 1930s, so popular it was made into a movie in 1944. The story's backdrop is of a woman charmed by a suave, sophisticated man who convinces her to marry him. He then systematically manipulates her into questioning her sanity, so he can place her in a sanitarium to steal her aunt's jewels. Consciously or unconsciously, gaslighting always has a goal. It is insidious and can be a silent, deadly form of continual abuse.

Gaslighting can be played out by politicians and political systems for political or financial gain, by cult leaders to keep their followers under control–even to death, in violent domestic relationships, and in something as innocuous as advertising. Control is not something any person generally gives away to another person on a whim. I don't know anyone who wakes up one day and says, "Hey, I think I'll completely give my power and dignity over to so-and-so today."

Dr. Robin Stern's book, *The Gaslight Effect: How to Spot and Survive the Hidden Manipulation Others Use to Control Your Life,*[5] was a valuable resource that helped validate my thought processes and rid me of the beliefs that I was not okay and that every situation was my fault. I came to realize I hadn't misunderstood all the time my dad and my first husband Ron said I did.

My father was always trying to make himself appear as a "good guy" with lots of money and giving generously within the community. He once spent most of his Christmas budget purchasing the famous honey baked hams from The Honey Baked Ham Company. He wanted only the best for leaders in his church, leaving minimal funds for anyone else's gifts. He didn't consider the feelings of anyone else in his family.

As I grew, I saw behaviors and attitudes demonstrating how my dad needed to appear so much more knowledgeable than me. After all, he was the parent, and I was the child. During my senior year in high school, he advised me to go to secretarial school, believing that as a girl, it was the only profession I could study and make a decent living. While it is true that this was a prevalent belief in society then, I had plans and dreams of my own but could not voice them because he would shoot each one out of the sky like a laser beam. If something didn't fit his paradigms, it wouldn't happen, and I was stupid to think it could.

When I married my first husband, I was desperate for love and attention, believing the lies my father wielded. I was also ripe for him to take the baton from where my dad had left off and continue gaslighting me.

How the Gaslighting Pattern Continued

During that first marriage, Ron would often agree to do something or go somewhere with our friends, yet when they arrived to leave with us, he would deny he had said yes in the first place. Then, he publicly made comments claiming I was the one who had said yes, not him, and I was "so stupid" and should have checked with him first. That was humiliating, but after our friends left, I would quietly talk to him. He would stick to his story, making me seriously question myself, my memory, and if I truly was that stupid.

One of the worst gaslighting he ever did was to blame his infidelity on me, as you'll remember from chapter six. I wrestled with that confession from Hong Kong for most of our married life.

Years later, after diving into Dr. Stern's book, I knew I was dealing with a quagmire of emotions from being gaslit during my youth and my first marriage. Not being a stranger to working with a therapist, I sought help from a professional. My therapist helped me see that in situations of gaslighting, the severity of the damage to one's self-esteem doesn't happen overnight. The problem is that gaslighting isn't always readily apparent until you begin to see the truth about someone you are in a relationship with. And it isn't always someone you have a romantic relationship with. Here's the important thing–it starts with someone you give a degree of authority to–and that someone takes it and runs with it, such as a boss who is always making derogatory comments about you in front of your coworkers.

End Results of Being a Gaslighting Victim

A gaslighter can get defensive toward us when we stand up for ourselves. Often, the only way to stop the gaslighting is to cease engaging in the conversation and the relationship altogether.

I met a woman named Casey at a networking event. I was struck by how much self-confidence she had. I was surprised when she told me she had been married to her second husband for about five years but had left when she realized he had been gaslighting her. When they met, he was considerate of her and her daughter. Her friends thought he was a great guy and a good match for her. Casey was smitten and considered herself fortunate to have met him. After they married, though, he was a different man behind closed doors.

On one occasion, Casey described to me that she was headed out the door to meet her friends, and he asked where she was going, told her she looked like a whore, and accused her of meeting another man. She was wearing something sleeveless yet respectful.

Over time, Casey began thinking of ending her own life, feeling so badly about herself after listening to all the criticism and accusations he threw at her. Casey doubted her sanity and questioned her abilities as a mother. With all the derogatory comments, Casey believed it would be best if she weren't alive anymore, but the thought that her daughter would have to live with her biological father was the only thing keeping her on the planet.

Fortunately, Casey's friends stood by her and suggested she get help, which she did. She slowly could stand up for herself with the encouragement of her support system. Casey told me she hadn't realized how warped her mind had gotten until she was out of the marriage. The woman I saw before me that day had undoubtedly rallied herself and came back to recognize her value as a mother to her child and a woman to the world.

Choosing to Stand Up and Walk Away

My friend, Sarah, shared with me the story of a relationship she had had with her friend, Mary. She had known Mary for over five years. They had met right after their divorces and talked on the phone daily to commiserate with each other.

Sarah went on to say she was confused about why her friend treated her the way she did. Dominating the conversation, or never wanting to do what Sarah wanted to do.

When Mary needed surgery, Sarah took a week off work to be at her friend's house to help out. Parking for guests was metered, so Sarah needed to feed the meter every two hours. One of Mary's neighbors noticed Sarah putting coins in the meter several times a day and asked her why she wasn't just parking in the garage across the street.

Sarah asked Mary about it. "You've seen me leave every couple of hours to move my car and feed the meters so I wouldn't get a ticket. Why didn't you say anything? I could have parked in the garage. That hurts my feelings, Mary."

Mary responded with a sideways glance, "I don't know why *your* feelings are hurt! It's not my job to protect you from getting a ticket."

"It's called considering other's feelings–and their pocketbook, Mary!" she fired back. "Someone who is here to help you."

One day Sarah called me and said, "I was listening to a podcast on the way to work this morning and heard about gaslighting. I had never heard the term before, so I looked it up. Do you realize Andy gaslit me the entire time we were married?" She was elated; she finally had an answer to her dilemma of not understanding how her ex-husband and Mary had treated her the way they did.

After reading an additional article online, it dawned on Sarah how similar the relationship with her friend Mary was to the one she had with her ex-husband. She began looking back at her friendship with Mary, discovering it had always been a one-sided commitment. Sarah always made concessions and realized Mary had taken advantage of the friendship. She remembered feeling belittled by Mary during most of their conversations. Sarah's words always got twisted, just as they had in her marriage.

After learning about gaslighting, Sarah started standing up for herself. That didn't go well because it didn't work in favor of Mary's goal. She ultimately decided to walk away from the relationship and friendship with Mary.

Are You Experiencing Gaslighting?

The following are listed in no order–nor do all of behaviors I have observed to indicate gaslighting always occur. Are you experiencing any of the following in one or more relationships?

- When engaging in a conversation with this person, do you feel like you are losing your mind?
- Do you go in argumentative circles both in your head or out loud?
- Are you second-guessing your decisions or memory?
- Are you apologizing and maybe not knowing why?
- Do you most often feel misunderstood?
- Are your words twisted around to the point where you are blamed for something you did not do–or not to the degree it is now portrayed?
- Are you having bursts of anger from the frustration of not being heard and then apologizing for your outburst?
- Are you experiencing weight gain or loss trying to please someone by using food to make yourself feel better?
- Are you being told blatant lies?
- Is someone denying they did or said something even though you have proof they did?
- Do they often tell you, "I'm just teasing; can't you take a joke?"
- Does it appear they are trying so hard to please you in front of others, but it's a different story behind closed doors?

What to Do to Move Beyond Gaslighting

There is good news if you have discovered that you have been gas-lit in one or more relationships. Awareness is always the first step. Congratulations if that is the case for you. You don't have to continue in the patterns you may have been taught as early as childhood. Now that you know more, do–or as in the case of gaslighting, *stop* doing the things that make you feel crazy with this person.

- Stop engaging in conversations and walk away from the discussion at hand whenever necessary. They begin to get the hint that gaslighting and lying will no longer work on them.
- Be consistent with your words, refusing to engage with them when the words they are spewing are trying to get you to continue with the conversation and to manipulate you into getting their way.
- Seek emotional support, either from friends, family, or a professional therapist. If the behavior is gaslighting, friends may not see what is truly happening. The person may appear perfectly normal–even charming when around your friends.
- Stand firm with your beliefs about what you saw or heard.
- Write things down in detail right after something happens. Possibly in a journal. It helps you to see more clearly when the emotions settle down, and you can review it with a clear mind.
- Stop apologizing when they tell you that you are mistaken or wrong.
- Don't second guess yourself if you decide to end the relationship for good. Stand fast in your resolve.
- Don't allow your feelings to be minimized.
- Do some journaling about your feelings, your thoughts, your dreams, and your desires so as not to lose yourself. You being *you* is vitally important.

Ultimate Gaslighting and Brainwashing

Because of the unique content in this chapter, I have added a special addition here. A fellow author, friend, and activist that I know has an incredible story that showcases how strong gaslighting can be and how challenging it was to break free.

Briell Decker was eighteen when she became the sixty-fifth wife of self-proclaimed prophet/leader of the FLDS Church (Fundamentalist Church of Jesus Christ of Latter-day Saints), Warren Jeffs.

I had the opportunity to sit down with Briell and ask her some questions. Here are the most powerful pieces of our interview.

Briell: The day Warren and I were married, my father was instructed to take me back to the house I was raised in. I thought it was weird, but I wasn't overly concerned. But the next day, my father was told to take me to a meeting Warren was officiating. As I sat waiting for it to begin, I looked around and saw over a dozen men, and leaders in the church, many of whom I loved and admired, waiting as well.

Warren soon walked to the front of the room and called out the names of the twelve men one by one and asked them to stand up. He proceeded to declare God told him they were no longer worthy to remain in the church because they were master deceivers. They were told to leave their homes and weren't allowed to see their wives or children ever again. They lost everything. I was horrified and saw a lot of red flags that day.

Me: Why would he do that?

Briell: It was a very common thing for the members of the church to be persecuted by the prophet because they didn't obey him. Warren was always saying God had instructed him to do these things.

Me: Was it then you began thinking you made a mistake by agreeing to marry Warren?

Briell: No. The next day I was directed to attend a second "special" meeting with Warren. He instructed me to take the children away from thirty of my sister wives who were living in the same home we all shared with Warren. I was to give them to other women temporarily. Warren told me he had been instructed by God that the wives were no longer worthy of being the children's mothers; even though they had given birth to them, they had to leave.

Me: That must have been devastating.

Briell: Families were being torn apart, the children were taken away from their mothers and given to another woman temporarily, and sometimes siblings were separated, never to be reunited. It was very devastating. After that, I made a commitment to myself I would do anything I could to protect the children from Warren.

Me: What did you do to protect the children?

Briell: I stood up for the children when I could to protect them and tried to stay away from Warren as much as I could because I didn't want to have children with him.

Me: How did you accomplish that?

Briell: I read books or found anything else to do so I would be anywhere where Warren wasn't. I gradually became pretty outspoken about how the children were being treated, so Warren sent me to other compounds to live. Those compounds were run by Warren's special confidants, men who followed his teaching to the letter.

Me: That's unbelievable.

Briell: After a time it got to the point I was unable to discern what was real and what was made up or who and what I could trust.

Me: Can you explain what you mean by "made" up?

Briell: Well, people left or were sent away, and later we would be told they had died in some accident, or no one ever heard from or saw them again after they were gone. I didn't know if the stories were real or not. I heard some man had jumped to his death off the edge of a cliff. We never knew for sure if maybe the stories were made up to scare us so we would obey. I lived in constant fear that one of two things would happen to me.

Me: What were those two things?

Briell: In the FLDS church, I could either be declared I was blood atonement worthy, meaning I had to die, *but* I could still go to Zion. Or I would be sent to a long-term psychiatric facility, losing all of my rights.

Me: How could they send you to a psychiatric unit? Were you given some kind of diagnosis they could use against you?

Briell: Former prophet Rulon Jeffs (Warren's father) sent men to medical school. After they graduated, they became the cult's doctors. I was given medication prescribed *by Warren*, who decided when the drug was to be given and when it was to be taken away. The doctors obeyed Warren's orders, fearing their families would be taken away for not obeying, so it could have been easily arranged. Warren's secret confidants told me I was worthy of blood atonement. I was always being told I had heard things wrong.

Me: You mentioned you were very outspoken. Was that the reason Warren had you moved around so much?

Briell: He controlled everyone and everything in the congregation. People obeyed because Warren told everyone God was giving him directions about everything. When church members no longer had any significant standing in the church, they were sent back to Short Creek where Warren no longer had an interest and ignored them. I planned to eventually be one of those people sent back to Short Creek.

Me: Was that where you were living when you escaped?

Briell: Yes, but before I got sent there, I was able to get myself sent to the big compound (the YFZ ranch) in Eldorado, Texas. I wanted to see for myself what was happening to the children at the ranch. I was there for about one and a half years when I let it be known I was no longer praying. My plan worked because I was taken to Short Creek by my brother, who was under the threat of being pronounced unworthy if he didn't take me to his house. It was there I was locked in solitary until I was able to remove the screws and climb out a window and escape.

Five years after their wedding, Warren was convicted of felony counts of child sexual assault, for which he is now serving a life sentence plus twenty years.[6]

Warren had the ability to gaslight his entire congregation of ten thousand members. He kept everyone in line by perpetuating the fear they would be declared unworthy of salvation and unable to go to Zion (their version of heaven) if they didn't obey. No one doubted Warren had the ear of God because he was the prophet, and it was believed he was receiving messages directly from Him, so Warren's world was rarely questioned. When the consequences were so devastating, others wouldn't dare make that same mistake.

Briell summarized the events after she escaped. This escape took place five years after their wedding in 2011.

By the time Briell had escaped, she had said she had been gaslit for so long with such intensity that she didn't know if she would even survive on the outside. She questioned her sanity many times. Still, she made the decision to continue to heal.

Briell was able to petition for ownership of a very large house located in Short Creek she and other sister wives had once shared with Warren. Briell now wanted to help other FLDS members who had escaped, giving them somewhere to go. She wanted something good to come from all they had been through.

In 2017, that house became The Dream Center. It provides a safe space for women and children escaping human trafficking and domestic violence. The Center offers free shelter, food, and life enrichment classes to its residents to directly support escaping abuse and finding strong and supportive footing for a new life–away from unhealthy, fixed beliefs and gaslighting.

> *"It's my dream to see this compound turned into a safe house and a refuge for victims-a place where they can grow, heal, get educated, and find their strength and happiness. They need a safe place surrounded by others who understand what they have been through and who can give them hope for a better tomorrow."*
> *—Briell Decker*

You will be able to read about her entire miraculous journey in detail in her soon-to-be-published book.

Final Thoughts

In my own life, I can see how the intensity of my relationships, beginning with my dad and then with Ron, increased over time. At the end of my marriage, I believe that the tendency for violence was there between us. When slamming doors wasn't satisfying enough, I took to throwing things in Ron's direction. I didn't care for how I began to act when my thoughts and feelings were discounted day after day, so it's easy to see how gaslighting can sometimes escalate into violence on either end. It's simply not healthy. It's important to note, however, that things did not change for me until I stood up for myself and quit engaging in any argument.

In my late thirties, Dad used his emergency key to come in and search through my son's desk for the paperwork for the new computer

Dad bought with the agreement my son would make the payments. Dad assumed it was going to cost him money because my son had quit his job, although he already been interviewed for a new one. My son fully intended to continue to cover the payments he had been faithfully making. I was livid when I got home and found out Dad had used his key to come in. There was an understanding the key was to be used only in an emergency. Dad tried to justify himself as he had for three decades. For the *very first time*, I looked him straight in the eye and said, "You know what, Dad? I don't have to listen to this. You're not going to twist my words around this time."

I turned on my heel and walked away. I finally took a stand for myself.

You can also pull yourself out of those toxic relationships too. Become important enough in your own life. You're not crazy. You're not stupid. You have value. Take the most essential steps above-especially seeing a knowledgeable therapist if needed-and demand your life back. Your very life may be at stake. Your happiness certainly is, and it's time to enjoy life with healthy people!

CHAPTER EIGHT

Becoming Mrs. Fixit

I know I can, I think I can . . . fix it, that is.
—Madison Frederick

A codependent relationship can go around in circles, but it also limits both people involved. The first time I heard the word "codependency" was when I started attending the Twelve Step Program in Alcoholics Anonymous after I divorced my husband, Ron. It is common to find this behavior in someone close to people struggling with addiction.

However, casting a wide net can garner other situations where, unfortunately, codependent relationships can also thrive. In the next chapter, I will share my experiences in my Twelve Step recovery program, where I discovered I had picked up many new learned behaviors. Still, codependency deserves a chapter of its own because it can lead to feelings of insanity if you don't get healthy.

Melody Beattie, the author of *Codependent No More: How to Stop Controlling Others and Start Caring For Yourself*,[7] provided life-changing information for me. She defines a codependent as a person who lets another person's behavior affect them and is obsessed with controlling that person's behavior.

Codependent people often look for things outside of themselves to feel better. They form relationships that are not healthy, believing the other person needs to be "fixed" or "helped" so the relationship can thrive. As a learned behavior whose purpose is to protect us from the emotions caused by hurt or trauma and focus on "helping" someone else, we don't have to look at ourselves.

Many kinds of relationships can be codependent: romantic, family, coworkers, and even friendships. Rescuing someone or solving someone's problem seems like a caring, supportive thing-perhaps even heroic-but it hinders your and the other person's growth and development.

Under the umbrella of codependency, I lost my self-identity and the ability to voice my desires and needs. At the beginning of my marriage to Ron, I desperately wanted to have a close relationship with him. Because of my upbringing and conditioning, I was taught that this meant I needed to put Ron first. I also needed to do my best to create a safe environment at our house.

Dr. Amy Johnson, the author of *The Little Book of Big Change: The No-Willpower Approach to Breaking Any Habit*,[8] states: "Common markers of codependency include extreme fear of the relationship ending, compulsive concern with the other person, self-doubt, and not having a sense of self outside the relationship."

Codependency *Is* a Habit

Over time, the codependent behaviors I developed became habits. For example, Ron loved to go camping and fishing. I didn't enjoy those activities primarily because of the cost of all the equipment and fees that weren't in the budget, and we didn't have money for; however, I convinced myself it was okay to spend the money and go anyway because, after all, he had grown up loving the Uinta Mountains in Utah. I believed I was being supportive.

Over my married years, I repeatedly focused on everything outside of myself. I neglected to feel any of my own emotions, swallowing them throughout my life because it was too painful to look at any hurt or disappointments. They were buried so deep that I wasn't even aware I needed to look at them.

When things went awry, I tried to fix my relationship with my husband, which meant "fixing Ron." I bought different clothes so he would be up to style even though he was comfortable with what he wore. I dragged us to the Marriage Encounter weekend designed to strengthen a Catholic marriage because "he" needed to learn to communicate his feelings with me. Never looked in the mirror at myself, not healing my wounded child inside. I returned to the same destructive behavior every time, thus relying on the habit of looking out for everyone else's wants and needs.

Transporting Myself from Enabling to Codependency

Enabling is a behavior that is a part of codependency. After Ron's "slip" with another woman, I convinced myself it *was* my fault because I had believed my marriage was better than it was. I swallowed the pain from his justification, and I bought into his reasoning hook, line, and sinker as to why he had gone home with the "barmaid" in the first place.

I reasoned that *I must not have been a good enough wife.* I convinced myself it was apparent Ron had needs that I wasn't satisfying, and his "gift" of a sex book proved it. I needed to up my performance in the bedroom, and if I did, our relationship would improve.

Because of my deep fear of being left alone, I made it my mission to fix our marriage. I had an excessive, all-consuming dependence on our relationship, hence the Marriage Encounter weekend.

I planned to make things easier for Ron. If he felt better about me and our marriage, our relationship would thrive. Unknowingly, I became a people pleaser for my husband and everyone in my life. I lost any sense of my authentic self. I put into action the most exemplary codependency behavior I knew. I became a chameleon, morphing into the version of what I believed Ron wanted.

Whenever Ron and I would argue, I put the kids to bed early so we could *talk* about it. I cooked a special dinner and planned the evening so Ron and I could have uninterrupted alone time to talk. However, I typically caved into Ron's justification for what he wanted, not solving anything.

On the outside, it could be said spending time talking through our problems was a healthy thing to do. However, spending as much time after the "special" dinner with Ron was detrimental to my relationship to my children. I put quality time with them on the back burner way too many times.

Fourteen years into the relationship, I was still trying to cater to his needs and repair our marriage. The worst part was that I didn't recognize the dynamics of codependency from the inside. I lived in a loveless marriage, not understanding how to be in a good partnership. I did the best I could but wasn't educated in the dynamics of relationships, nor what was healthy or unhealthy.

Using the traits listed below, on a scale from one to ten, how frequent are these habits in your life? Make a note of your answers on the note pages provided at the end of the book.

- Are you a people pleaser?
- Do you lack the capabilities to set healthy boundaries?
- Do you have self-esteem challenges?
- Are you a caretaker because you believe people cannot care for themselves?
- Do you have poor communication skills?
- Are you afraid to ask for what you need or want?
- Are you loyal no matter what?
- Do you put aside your interests and do what others want?
- Do you refuse to give up? Even when everyone else has?
- Do you believe it is "unselfish" to dedicate yourself to the well-being of others?
- Do you self-sacrifice frequently, putting everyone first with a martyr mentality?
- Do you minimize, alter, or deny how you truly feel?

When I assessed these eleven questions over three decades ago, I ranked my numbers at an eight or higher on each one. Fortunately, that's in the past. That's not to say that these traits don't resurface now and again; life is a journey. I feel blessed to say today that my numbers more frequently rank around one–and two, on occasion.

When I catch myself in those patterns, I make sure to take a look at why so I can carefully watch for future behaviors to be nipped in the bud before they bloom into nightmares. It took me a while to get there because we often only see what we want to see.

Becoming aware of codependent behaviors is an excellent way for you to start changing and recovering from the insanity of codependency and into a more extraordinary life of joy and freedom.

Shifts after Divorce

In a divorcing family, tensions can become relatively high. Shifts will take place to survive. When Ron and I divorced, I didn't have him to "fix" any longer. I turned my focus toward my relationship with my children. However, I still carried within me the inability to set healthy boundaries and unawareness of my true self.

There was such a driving force within me to have a relationship with my children and other human beings that I forgot to have a relationship with myself. I became enmeshed with my children, not having any clear boundaries in our relationships. Enmeshment was when I clearly felt my children's pain as if it were my own, and that's what drove me to go out of my way to make them *feel* better.

Buying special treats or taking them out to dinner and a movie are great examples. In a twisted way, I exhibited the same underlying behavior when I prepared a "special" meal for Ron so we could talk in my attempt to protect our marriage from falling apart. I became vested in building a close relationship with my children for fear of being left alone.

As I had learned at an early age, I felt I *needed* to invest time and money to have a relationship with someone. I would buy them a scheduled treat, like a weekly Slurpee from the 7-11.

Reflecting on that time in my life, I can see how my behavior could have been very confusing to my children. I told the kids money was tight, and we couldn't afford extras, but then I would pull money seemingly out of the air–the same money I had told them we didn't have for a treat or entertainment-to ease any emotional pain I saw them experiencing.

As Dr. Johnson points out, I couldn't put healthy boundaries for my children, let alone myself, to keep from spending money I didn't have. I couldn't follow the budget I created for myself because my priority was my children's short-term happiness, and counteracting my severe worry of loss of my children in the future, so I kept trying to buy a harmonious life.

Opportunities for Support

Al-Anon is an organization that primarily focuses on the recovery of a person who has a friend or relative in their life struggling with alcohol addiction. There is another recovery program born out of Alcoholics Anonymous called Codependency Anonymous (CODA), where the emphasis is on codependency recovery. It can apply to different relationships: romantic, family, work associates, or even friendship.

Gently Breaking Free from Codependency

Below are some healthy ways to break free of codependency. They are tried-and-true methods that genuinely help build great boundaries, allow for healing, and help you to see things more clearly in your relationships when instituted one at a time.

- **Break the habit of doing things in a codependent manner.** Learn how to express your very own wants and needs. At first, this may feel selfish, but you are filling your well so that your cup doesn't run dry. You're also modeling this for others in your life.
- **Stand up for yourself by saying:** "I love you, and I love me too. I am doing what I need to do for myself, so I show up balanced and healthy."
- **Develop a spiritual practice.** It doesn't need to be based on religious teachings. The time spent with this can deepen your relationship with yourself. You may also find that there is a force bigger than you.
- **Plan to spend time alone to restore your energy and sense of well-being**.
- **Love yourself** by being gentle and having compassion for yourself.
- **Monitor yourself when your inner thoughts pop up,** prompting you to take action to protect a relationship—speaking to yourself in a calm, kind, and constructive voice.
- **Develop trust that you can count on yourself.**

- **Pursue your own passions.**
- **When emotions rise** to the surface, instead of stuffing them down, **try to identify where in your body you feel them.** Inhale deeply and visualize your breath entering that part of your body. On the exhale, imagine the discomfort of the emotion leaving.
- **Practice mirror work**, spending three or four minutes looking yourself straight in the eye, repeat the following mantra:
  - (*Insert your name*) I love you.
  - You've got this.
  - Add any other positive thoughts about yourself.

Last Thoughts

Changing unhealthy patterns may feel uncomfortable at first, but it gets easier. There is a saying that goes, "My old skin isn't comfortable anymore, and the new skin doesn't quite fit yet either."

It is essential to recognize that your wants and needs *are* important. You can't always walk away from a relationship, but you can stop letting the relationship run you. You deserve to have peace and harmony in your life. Actions I took:

- I set the intention to simply find a centered, calm place to access my inner guidance.
- I listened to my inner guidance and found inner truth, which gave me greater confidence, clarity, and peace. It will also helped me to let go of control and be less reactionary, despite what's happening all around me. It's *not* your responsibility to fill the needs of others or bandage their emotional wounds.
- As often as possible, I celebrate the new me. All things are possible, even though it can feel awkward and selfish at first. I have faith you can find freedom from codependency.

CHAPTER NINE

My Twelve Step Segway to Self-Awareness

Don't set yourself on fire trying to keep others warm.
—Penny Reid

This codependent behavior created the need for my excessive emotional and psychological investment in my relationship with Ron. I couldn't face another abandonment. I clung to my marriage so tightly that my fingers were bloody.

I struggled daily with anger, close-mindedness, being overly critical and judgmental of others, perfectionism, control, resentment, and having the mindset of victimhood. These all created massive problems in my relationships. I would learn that these are called "character defects," or imperfections and flaws in character. My character defects precipitated behaviors that impacted my relationships.

Fortunately for me, along with an understanding of these character defects, it was revealed that there are tools to help me overcome and cope with all of my human flaws that I still use today. Progress, not perfectionism, became my new mantra. I still choose to give myself the grace to be human.

The kids and I lived in Utah for almost three years while Ron was in California, living on an aircraft carrier. Three months after Ron left the navy, things finally came to a head with my marriage to Ron. With great courage, I filed for divorce. I found strength in my newfound freedom, gathering up the needed strength to move forward with my life–even though I was scared shitless about how I would support myself and my children.

A friend at work suggested I look into the Al-Anon program to help me deal with my emotions that were still raw around the history of Ron's drinking. I thought about it, but I told myself if Ron would have just quit *his* drinking, *I* wouldn't have any more problems. I told myself my marriage was over so, and I didn't think I needed to go to Al-Anon. I took my friend's suggestion and went to my first meeting.

It's been said that the teacher appears when the student is ready. *My* teacher showed up as the entire staff of the "University of Lived Wisdom" professors who practiced the Twelve Steps of Alcoholics Anonymous.

I was emotionally loaded for bear, ready to blame everyone who I believed caused my misery in life. I showed up for that first meeting kicking and screaming because I resented the reason I even needed to go in the first place. It wasn't me that had the problem–or so I thought in the beginning. I thought *if Ron had just changed, I wouldn't have had these problems.* I had been drowning emotionally for years but was so busy surviving that I didn't notice.

So, on a Wednesday in the fall of 1986, I pulled into the parking lot of the Alano Club, a place where AA and Al-Anon meetings are held, in a suburb of Salt Lake City. Several people were standing around outside talking and smoking cigarettes. When I walked past them, I grimaced. I was reminded that our house always smelled like a dirty ashtray because of Ron's smoking. And I knew my clothes would stink the rest of the day.

The fact that the building had once been a church triggered me. It brought bitter memories and disappointment when my dad blew me off as a young teen when I requested he take me to church because I wanted to recreate a lifestyle I loved when living with my grandparents.

A sign just inside the door directed me to a room on the second floor, which had once been used as the cultural hall, a room for group activities. I sat on a gray metal folding chair in the back, scooting as far from the front as possible. Folding my arms across my chest as if to protect myself. I wasn't taking a chance of something rubbing off on me from one of *those* people.

That day someone was celebrating the fifth anniversary of their recovery in AA. Traditionally, this is when someone shares their personal story of how and why they started attending meetings–and for many, for the first time, they start learning how to be healthy instead of living life as an addict.

At the end of the meeting, everyone stood and held hands while the Serenity Prayer was recited, ending with the declaration, "Keep coming back. It works when you work it." But first came the prayer:

> *God grant me the serenity to accept the things I cannot change,*
> *The courage to change the things I can,*
> *And the wisdom to know the difference.*

The second sentence brought tears to my eyes. It was the closest I had come to a spiritual experience in over ten years.

A slim man with an infectious smile approached me with an outstretched hand, offering me a tissue. He introduced himself. I will call him Raymond because of the rule to protect his anonymity. He told me he was what was called a "double-dipper." As an alcoholic, he attended AA meetings and went to Al-Anon meetings because of his relationships. He shared it had been very beneficial because his spouse was an alcoholic. Raymond offered me his copy of the book *One Day at a Time in Al-Anon*. A daily reader that is taken from the principles of Alcoholics Anonymous. He invited me to an Al-Anon meeting the very next day.

At my first "official" meeting, I was intrigued as I listened to a woman who shared her story and I saw how similar our experiences had been. She spoke of the many sleepless nights waiting for her husband to get home, never knowing if he was okay or not. She talked about all the fights she'd had with him because of his drinking and how emotionally drained she always felt before going to Al-Anon meetings. Then she spoke of how free she felt now and full of this thing called . . . joy.

I started going to Al-Anon regularly. The life situations shared in meetings resonated deeply within me. And when I shared, I didn't feel judged about anything I said. I felt unconditional acceptance, even though in the beginning, I still blamed all of my problems on Ron and my dad.

I eventually came to understand that *I* was powerful. I had a piece in creating my misery! I needed to acknowledge *my* actions before I could ease my emotional anguish. It soon became crystal clear that it would be in my best interest to focus on myself. I needed to stop focusing all of my attention on my efforts I had taken to fix Ron's problems in the past, feelings, wants, and needs–and quit minimizing my own. It was time to stop worrying obsessively about everybody in my family and concentrate on my stuff.

Reset Button

Using any coping device or substance regularly will feed an addiction. A few examples are drugs, alcohol, sex, gambling, pornography, shopping, binge-watching Netflix, and food. I believe we are all addicted to something. Practicing the Twelve Steps of Alcoholics Anonymous can offer someone so much more than a life of staying clean and sober. Not that it's any small feat to accomplish. It doesn't matter what the "drug" of choice is. Although I didn't know it at the time, I had become the perfect codependent Al-Anon, and my drug of choice was food, although I wouldn't realize that until much later in life.

We use substances to numb pain, usually stemming from some sort of trauma we don't want to look at.

Six months after sitting in the rooms attending an Al-Anon meeting, I met Karen Q. She was an extremely bright, compassionate woman. When Karen smiled, she made people feel at ease. She was forty-five when I met her, and I was thirty-six. The life situations Karen shared in meetings were something that resonated deeply with me. After one meeting on a Saturday in late winter, I invited Karen to meet me at a Village Inn for a piece of pie and coffee. I wanted to ask her if she would be my Al-Anon sponsor. Karen agreed to meet me.

I felt a little nervous and intimidated to ask her because Karen had already been in the program for multiple years. I wanted to work my way through the Twelve Steps, to be accountable to someone else. However, that meant telling her all the details of my life. I would be laying myself completely bare, out in the open. That meant there was the distinct possibility of being hurt or abandoned once again.

When I arrived at the Village Inn, I was as nervous as a cat on a hot tin roof. My emotions were all over the place. I got there well before Karen did. The hostess sat me in a booth. Feeling small in the worn, brown imitation leather, and the backs of the bench were too tall for me to see around.

Part of me wanted to ensure Karen saw me when she got there, while the seated other part wanted to run away quickly. This was a massive step for me, risking such vulnerability. I had been around the Al-Anon program long enough to know I would have to *own* every piece of my story . . . and that's precisely what frightened me. I waited for Karen because I *knew* it would empower me to have a sponsor.

As soon as I saw Karen walking toward the booth, flashing a huge smile, acknowledging she had seen me, I felt all the nervousness and intimidation disappear. That night she agreed to be my sponsor, and we shared more deeply than ever.

I believe God brought Karen into my life so I could learn about myself and my relationships. After leaving my marriage, I let the steam out of my collar and breathed. I didn't know it then, but I would learn to love and allow myself to be loved for the first time since I had lived with my grandma. I discovered that my and Karen's childhoods were very similar, as our married lives ended in divorce, among other things.

"Can you believe I wasn't allowed to sing when I was younger?" I asked her, shaking my head, remembering riding in the backseat of our white Volvo as a kid, forbidden to sing "Jingle Bells," and being yelled at by my mom.

With a faraway look on her face, Karen replied, "I know what you mean. I wasn't allowed to play anywhere except in my room because my dad said I was too noisy!"

"Well, I don't know if I even know how to play," I said in reflection.

Out of the ether came a thought from the Divine. "Well, why don't we *just learn how* to play?" I said, flashing a grin that would have challenged that of a Cheshire cat.

"That's a great idea!" Karen agreed, and I loved seeing her face light up as well.

From then on, Karen and I often rode to meetings together. Soon our energy was so contagious that, along with other friends from our Twelve Step group, we went out together for what's called the meeting after the meeting, usually at a Village Inn. That's where we shared stories and laughter with pearls of wisdom over coffee, chili cheese fries, and soda. It was at those gatherings I slowly began to open up to others and show the real me.

With Karen's guidance I began working the Twelve Steps.

What Are the Twelve Steps?

A fellowship program was born when two men, Bill W. and Dr. Bob, came together to help each other stay sober. If you're unfamiliar with the Twelve Steps, they are worth familiarizing yourself with, no matter what kind of healing journey you are on. It's something that may serve you and someone you love. The program has been around for nearly a century, and its influence is now felt worldwide through multiple generations. For more information about Alcoholics Anonymous and the Twelve Steps, see resources in the back of book.

After doing some work on each step, it is customary to go over them with your sponsor. It did take me some time to work through the steps and wasn't always easy. These are the things I did for myself for each one.

Step One. While reflecting on my life, I was able to recognize *how unmanageable* my life had become. I set boundaries for myself and my children.

Step Two. I had been struggling with the whole concept of God, or higher power. While journaling, I was able resolve my confusion enough to realize *there is a power greater than myself.*

Step Three. After completing step two, it was reasonable for me to *turn my life and my will over* to my higher power.

Step Four. I had been working with Karen and sharing what I believed were my shortcomings. Especially in regard to many of my relationships. It was time to look at myself and to *take a moral inventory.*

Step Five. I *admitted* to my higher power, and to Karen, the exact nature of the unkind things I had done in the past.

Step Six. I became *ready* to turn them over to my higher power for their removal.

Step Seven. I then *gave* them over to my higher power so all of my shortcomings could be removed.

Step Eight. I took a look at the list of those I had harmed so I could make my amends.

Step Nine. Whenever it was possible, I made my amends in person.

Step Ten. I need to continually take inventory of my shortcomings, and then make amends if necessary.

Step Eleven. Using prayer and meditation, I sought to understand my higher power on a more conscious level.

Step Twelve. After doing all of this work, I made the commitment to share this process with others and practice the principles of the steps in my life.

Working the steps is a process I have taken many times since the first time I worked them with my sponsor Karen. Each time I go through them, I learn something more about myself. I can then stay honest with myself. As I walk my journey and hopefully grow, there is always life events and circumstances to live through; after all, I am living this human experience just like you.

In addition to Alcoholics Anonymous, other Twelve Step programs focusing on other specific issues with meetings are available. To name just a few of the sixty programs:

- Gamblers Anonymous[9]
- Overeaters Anonymous[10]
- Cocaine Anonymous[11]
- Adult Children of Alcoholics[12]
- Debtors Anonymous[13]
- Narcotics Anonymous[14]
- Codependent[15]

According to an Al-Anon Family Groups member survey conducted in 2021, there are currently over 24,000 Al-Anon groups and nearly 1,500 Alateen groups meeting in 118 countries.

I attribute a chunk of my growth to the fact that I went to that first Al-Anon meeting over thirty years ago. After Karen passed away in 1994 from an illness, it was too difficult for me to attend Al-Anon. I turned my focus to learning other tools. I studied and got certifications for modalities related to energy work—reiki, feng shui, and EFT[16] (Emotional Freedom Technique) tapping, among others.

Shortly before writing this book, I began attending a Twelve Step meeting again via Zoom, which focuses on my food addiction program. I started working on the steps again. I show up for meetings within the fellowship because I always hear things that help me to keep my addictions at bay. I continue to learn more about myself and my addictive personality, which strengthens me positively.

I consider myself an entirely different person because of my Twelve Step journey. It took some time to see the difference in myself, but I know this: change *is* possible, though not overnight. It has taken years to get where I am today.

What I've Learned:

I developed a spiritual practice that doesn't have anything to do with religion. While honoring my higher power, I am also honoring myself. Each morning I spend time with Him. Meditation and consistently checking with myself have helped me to find my truth. I sit in silence and listen for my inner guidance.

It's important to seek support if you have an addiction problem, either from friends or from a therapist who is familiar with self-improvement and is on a path looking to improve their own life. As humans, we need connections and a sense of belonging to some sort of tribe when we become lonely, overwhelmed, and confused with life.

When I get Hungry, Angry, Lonely, or Tired (HALT), I stop to determine my needs. This has become a key ingredient to my happiness. When I know my needs, I can ask for the support that best serves me. When I am providing service to others, not only does it help another, but it also feeds my soul. That is the reason I am writing this book.

Learning to be okay with disappointment or change helps me stay in the present moment. There are always uncertainties and unknowns in life. I've learned to adjust my perspective and find joy in the unexpected!

Last but not least, I know the importance of releasing my attachment to outcomes. Detaching with love brought sanity into my life.

Jan. 2 entry–Courage to Change-One Day at a Time, Al-Anon.

While these loved ones may not meet our expectations, it is our expectations, not our loved ones, that have let us down.

CHAPTER TEN

There Is More to Play Than Just Playing

Sing unto him a new song; play skillfully with a loud noise.
—Psalm 33:33

If I told you there was a way to improve your relationships and increase your feelings of well-being with play, would you be interested? In my own life, I discovered that when I allowed myself to be fully enveloped in a full belly roll laugh, I released trapped emotions from my past. Laughter, play, and letting things go are critical to my happiness.

In previous chapters, I have discussed the traumas and the different effects I felt and how they influenced the behaviors I created as a way to protect myself. For many people affected or traumatized by events, it's natural to look outside of ourselves to find the answers. However, when you begin to heal enough, you recognize how the responsibility for your joy and happiness is yours and yours alone. In this chapter, I make suggestions that can help you regain that personal power too.

We all deserve to be happy, regardless of the past. When you take responsibility for your peace and happiness, the learned behaviors you created to survive can be laid to rest.

Inner-Child Work

At an Al-Anon meeting, someone shared how John Bradshaw's PhD work had helped them process their wounded child. I purchased his book, *Homecoming: Reclaiming and Championing Your Inner Child.*[17] I took his profound teachings about reclaiming my childhood to heart.

I was so impressed that I signed up for a live workshop of Bradshaw's. During a guided meditation, he took us on a journey to a safe place. We were instructed to imagine ourselves at the age of three to five years old. Then we were invited to have someone from the past in a chair across from us that we thought didn't hear us as a child.

Following his instructions, I began talking to my dad about the mistreatment my mom had inflicted on me when doing my chores every Saturday. For the first time, I confronted Dad as I would have done if I had had the opportunity as a six-year-old about never being there for me. Relief came when I experienced an outpouring of grief, sadness, and even anger through the tears I had kept locked up inside my body for decades.

When I looked through the lens of my inner child's eyes and evaluated the relationship with my dad the way Bradshaw taught us, I could rewrite the end of the story. It is a way of showing up as the parent to my inner child and to reparent myself.

During the conclusion of the workshop, Bradshaw recommended continuing to have a dialogue with my inner child, citing that the use of a proxy as my child could be helpful. When I walked out of the workshop, it felt like a huge boulder was lifted from my shoulders!

That evening I did the exercise again and I rewrote the ending to the story of the day at Black Rock and the swimming pool, resulting in the little girl inside feeling loved and cared for.

The day after Bradshaw's workshop, while on our way to a Twelve Step meeting, I told my best friend, Karen, about my success at the workshop. "I wasn't sure when we started the meditation that I would be able to confront my dad," I admitted. "But I did it, and it feels so good!"

Karen looked at me with raised eyebrows and responded, "I don't know why you didn't think you could confront him; you've been doing some great healing work with yourself."

Sheepishly, I responded, "Well, we both know how much emotional baggage I have around my relationship with Dad!" We both laughed.

"I think I'd like to try the technique," Karen said, now curious.

"I was intrigued with the whole concept of inner-child work using a proxy," I said. "I want to get a stuffed bear to use as mine. Do you want to go to a toy store with me when I can pick her out?"

A huge grin appeared across Karen's face. "I'd love to get something for myself too! I'm not sure what to pick out yet . . . " Then she added, "Once we pick out our new 'kids,' let's get a piece of our favorite pie."

We went to a specialty toy store in the mall to find our proxies. As I wandered through the store, a box fell from the shelf, landing right in my arms. She was a stuffed bear with wheat-colored fur and a big patchwork heart stitched on her chest.

Little did I know that she would sit on a shelf in my office many years later, adorned with a brown straw hat with a flower wreath on her head. There she would sit, ready to assist my clients to fearlessly take on the process of starting their inner-child work.

Karen found George Albert, a black gorilla holding a banana in his hand for her proxy, which she showed off with a grin. We were being taught that every event or trauma that has happened to us gets stored on a cellular level, both positive and negative memories. We were both on our way to finding and repairing those negative stored emotions within us and making the best use of the positive ones.

Incorporating Our Newfound Playfulness

Even though Karen and I did quite a bit of serious recovery work, we always made time to laugh and have a great time. My spirit was always lifted when I took the time to play and be goofy. There is a natural way to find a higher sense of peace by creating our own "happy" hormones. I hadn't even heard of such a thing until I learned how important it was to create happiness for myself. What I discovered for myself is that *I'm happy when I play, and I play when I'm happy.*

With this adventurous spirit, Karen and I walked throughout Liberty Park in Salt Lake City, admiring the trees and gardens on many Saturdays. Often, we brought our newly purchased stuffed companions along for the ride. Our adventures allowed us to be ourselves without judgment and were very healing. Here we were, nearly middle-aged women acting like five-year-olds! It was the elixir of life for our souls.

In May of 1990, Karen talked me into going to a party. Her request was so far out of character. Karen was somewhat shy about having conversations with men in a party environment. I was surprised when she said she wanted to go.

"You have dragged me to many events for Parents Without Partners; an organization for single parents, you could at least do this for me!" she said in a pleading voice.

I didn't want to go because most of the men in that crowd were only interested in one-night stands. I wasn't too keen about being on some man's menu. I would much rather have gone bowling. That seemed so much more fun than going to a stuffy party.

But, in the end, I agreed to go. After all, I love to dance. It was there I met my soulmate, John. He shared with me that he hadn't wanted to attend the party either but decided to go at the last minute. I adamantly believe this was divinely orchestrated on many fronts.

That evening I learned that John had retired from the army. He offered to help me get a check from the navy from my marriage to Ron that I was entitled to from my divorce. John made a phone call the next day, and I received my check the next week! He became my knight in shining armor for two good reasons. The first was because, until that moment, I had never felt listened to and heard by any man. The second was that John was different. He was unique, and my willingness to play brought me to him.

When I think about John after our first official date, a smile still crosses my lips.

Creating Our Own Happiness

We all can create happiness. Some marvelous chemical substances called "happy hormones" can help us. They can promote feelings like pleasure, joy, and love. All emotions are actually chemical reactions in the brain.

What does play have to do with the happy hormones, you may ask? Once I became aware that there was something I could do to empower myself to increase these chemical substances in my brain, I used these techniques to bring my mood back up, thus alleviating stress. I learned that when these hormones are low or depleted, we can have challenges emotionally, physically, and spiritually.

The following information I have provided is based on my understanding of these powerful hormones we all have access to naturally. I suggest you choose one or two exercises or tips daily to increase your happy hormones or simply when you need to shift an emotional response. Here are the happy hormones:

Serotonin
- Helps balance mood and promote feelings of well-being.

Dopamine
- The "feel good" hormone. It plays a role of feeling happiness, pleasure, and reward.

Oxytocin
- Not technically a "happy" hormone, it's role in promoting social interaction may help you feel positive emotions.

Endorphins
- Your body's natural painkillers, they help you overcome stress or discomfort.

Actions to Take to Increase These Hormones

Using any of the methods below may help relieve an incredible amount of anxiety and stress while boosting your serotonin, dopamine, oxytocin, and even endorphins. I suggest choosing one or two at a time and considering trying something new if you feel comfortable doing so.

- Go outside in the sun. It can boost both endorphins and serotonin levels. Ten to fifteen minutes a day is an excellent place to start. This can even be done when the sun isn't shining by using a bright therapy lamp.
- Hug yourself. It increases serotonin.
- Using essential oils are powerful tools that can be used in three different ways: diffuse, applied topically, or by ingesting (with a

few exceptions). The olfactory system is the most powerful sense we have. There are six million receptors in a human nose.

- Warning: When using citrus oils, be mindful of skin exposure to the sun. Compounds known as furanocoumarins, found in citrus oils, significantly increase UV sensitivity.
- Watch a comedy movie or listen to a comedian. Laughter always makes me feel better.
- Exercise.
- Meditate.
- Listening to music cranked up while doing dishes or cooking is my jam that continuously improves my mood.
- Having sex creates endorphins.
- Owning a pet such as a dog or a cat is a great way to increase serotonin and oxytocin levels for you and your dog. Playing with them creates the desire to have more opportunities for even more! Have you noticed a dog that doesn't know when it is time to quit playing fetch? I have; my arm gets tired long before my dog Abby wants to quit.
- Get a massage.
- Sing.
- Practicing gratitude activates the brain to release these feel-good chemicals.
- Forest bathing, known as "*shinrin-yoku*"[18] in Japan, is so effective that it has been adapted into the work culture. They offer eco-antidotes to the tech-boom burnout and to inspire people to reconnect and ultimately protect the country's forests. Take advantage of what they have learned! While sitting in any woodsy area, wearing comfortable clothing, conscientiously immerse yourself in the forest's sights, sounds, and smells. This will effectively assist the body in bringing balance to your energy.
- The forest offers natural oils, and when we breathe and partake of the scents, they quickly lower blood pressure and increase happy hormones.

Taking Things to a Deeper Level

Harvard conducted a study lasting over seventy-five years regarding human happiness. Starting in 1938 with 724 male volunteers, it increased to 2,000 people when the wives and family members were included. As of 2015, sixty of these original men are still alive and participating in the study. The major takeaway they discovered is that the key to attaining happiness in life is to be socially connected with family, friends, and community to help cultivate good relationships and emotional health.[19]

Stress or dealing with stressful situations and events will cause a drop in dopamine and serotonin production, ultimately affecting your mood.

Issues with our hormones in what we humans call "moods" can lead to depression, low self-esteem, relationship challenges, many other problems, and other health concerns. Just spending time with some-one you care about can help boost oxytocin production. This can help increase closeness and positive relationships, making you feel better about yourself all the time.

In summary, the human body creates many of its very own happy hormones. By recognizing that you are the creator of your happiness and making essential but significant changes, you can rise from depression and anxiety into more essential periods of play, joy, and even bliss.

CHAPTER ELEVEN

Let Go and Let God

Grief is itself a medicine.
—William Cowper

G rief comes because of many reasons. Here are a few:

1. The loss of a friendship.
2. The loss of a job or career.
3. The loss of any kind of label with which you have identified.
4. The loss of self.
5. Loss due to a divorce.
6. Death of a loved one.

After my dear friend Karen, my cohort in "crime" or play passed away, I expected everyone to miss her as much as I did. Why was the world still turning? Didn't our mutual friends remember how special a woman she was? I was infuriated with these people because shortly after she died, they all appeared to have simply moved on. I was experiencing what is commonly thought of as the first stage of grief: anger.

The truth of the matter is that anger is an emotion that masks. It often comes out as a result of *false evidence appearing real (or FEAR)*. I wasn't really angry; I was afraid of being left alone. I wouldn't have a girlfriend to share the joy of life with any longer, to tell all my girl stuff secrets, and to grow with. I didn't know how I was going to function without her.

After Karen passed, I thought back on some of my best memories with her, and how things eventually went south when she got sick. I remembered how one day, in a dollar store, I found a pair of sunglasses with red diamond-shaped frames. On a whim, I bought two pairs. I presented them to Karen on our way to an Al-Anon meeting. We put them on, and with the windows rolled down, we danced in our seats to one of my favorite songs, *Get Outta My Dreams, Get Into My Car,* sung by Billy Ocean. It was so much fun to see the looks we got from other drivers, especially when we stopped at a light.

From then on, when we found some goofy-looking sunglasses, we each bought two pairs. We discovered all kinds of different colors and shapes. Some were round, square, and even some had sparkles on them. Imagine the frames Elton John wears, and you get the gist! And that was how we rolled.

Just three years later into our friendship, Karen was having digestion problems. She had several appointments with the doctor. Over a period of five months, he ordered all kinds of tests; he even had her change her diet. The results of all the tests were inconclusive, and a different diet seemed to not make any difference at all. Dr. Smith then ordered a biopsy of the intestine because colon cancer ran in her family.

The night before her procedure, I visited her in the hospital. While we were talking, Karen mentioned that some ladies she had met through the Twelve Step meetings were coming to do another reiki treatment to help her relax in preparation for her surgery.

"What is *reiki?*" I asked. I had never heard of it.

Just as she was about to explain, the three women walked through the door. They had her lie on her back, fully covered in her hospital gown and blanket. I watched as Karen closed her eyes. One of the women scooted the bed out from the wall far enough to position herself above Karen's head. I stood up to excuse myself, thinking they might need privacy.

"Please, stay. I want to talk to you afterward," Karen asked softly.

That's when the three women positioned themselves strategically around the bed. One woman worked on Karen's upper body, one in her midsection, with the third at her feet. As I watched them work, I was dumbfounded by what I witnessed. It was as if they had used a wide squeegee starting at the top of Karen's head, moving down toward her feet, releasing all the tension from her body. The woman who was working in Karen's midsection turned and saw my awe. She asked, "Do you want to come and help us?"

"I know nothing about reiki," I replied.

With a smile on her face, she instructed me. "Just put your hands on Karen's knees like this. I'm sure it will be of great help."

As soon as my hands touched Karen's knees over her blanket, I felt a surge of energy leave my hands and go into her knees. Taken aback, I immediately pulled my hands off Karen's body and stared at the palms of my hands. *How can this be? I don't even know what I'm doing, but I think there is something to this thing called reiki!*

Karen and I spoke briefly afterward, and she mentioned feeling just as I had witnessed– the tension had left, and she told me how prepared she felt for the next morning's procedure. I no longer felt anxious about what she would be going through the next day. I intended to check around and find someone to officially learn from. However, my plans were cut short by a phone call five days later.

The Biopsy That Changed Everything

"Can you come with me tomorrow to my appointment?" Karen asked. "Doctor Smith has the results of my biopsy."

My stomach felt like it traveled to my throat. *Uh oh, this doesn't sound good. Karen never asks for help with things like this!*

During the appointment, the doctor explained how he had found a tumor between Karen's small intestine and colon. He wanted to get her scheduled for surgery by the end of the week, and Karen agreed.

After the surgery was finished, the surgeon stepped into the waiting room, looking for me. Dr. Smith told me the tumor was the size of a grapefruit, but he thought they had gotten it all. Still, he was ordering radiation and a round of chemotherapy to be on the safe side.

Just in case. Yeah, right!

It felt like I had been punched in the gut. Momentarily, I made it all about me. *What am I going to do when she's gone?* As the surgeon left the room, I plopped into the chair, almost knocking it over, then put my head in my hands and sobbed.

Karen completed radiation and a regimen of chemotherapy. Once again, Karen asked if I would accompany her to her doctor's appointment to get an update. On a spring day in May of 1994, I slipped our favorite pairs of sunglasses into my pocket in hopes it would lighten the dark energy we were both feeling. I drove to her house to pick her up.

Arriving at the building, we got on the elevator and rode to the third floor, each in our own thoughts. Holding hands for support, we walked into an exam room. Dr. Smith clipped the film up on the screen so we could see the image of Karen's liver. He pointed out how much of the organ was now black. My heart fell. Apparently, cancer had not only taken over the colon but had made its way into the liver. I fought back the tears and attempted to put on a brave face for Karen's sake. I don't think I fooled her at all.

Karen got her affairs in order, then flew to Boston to see her daughter, and then to Denver to see her brother. We had agreed to meet in Denver to do some playing, but she called and canceled. When she returned, I clearly saw why she needed to use a wheelchair because she was so weak. Due to her rapid decline, Karen requested her AA community to have people just come and sit with her so she wouldn't be alone. As summer passed quickly, it was obvious it was only a matter of days. In the wee hours of the morning of September 4, 1994, I was honored to hold Karen's hand as she took her last breath.

We held a celebration of life service in Murray Park, with over one hundred people in attendance. I felt emotionally supported by so many of our mutual friends. But after the funeral, it was a different story. When I went to an Al-Anon meeting, no one appeared to be missing her as much as I was and I got angry. At least I didn't see anyone openly grieving–not how I thought people should be, anyway. I retreated deep into myself.

I wasn't ready to accept Karen's death. Even after three months' time, I was still struggling with sleeping through the night. Here I was without my best friend; I felt lost. My husband did his best to comfort me, but I continued to feel devastated.

Since leaving my grandmother's house at a young age, Karen was the first person I had ever let my guard down low enough to allow myself to feel unconditionally loved and accepted. Not only for who I was but *how* I was.

Karen's friendship opened me up to meeting and marrying the "man of my dreams," which was an incredible blessing. I had more work to do to accept his love as deeply and unconditionally as I had with Karen. I sank into a deep depression and quit attending my Al-Anon meetings. It was too painful for me to sit in those rooms.

Still, something had to change. The only tangible thing I had of Karen was her copy of the Big Book, and her stuffed gorilla George Albert. I didn't realize until much later that she had given me so much more. She had blazed a trail for me to have the ability to give and accept love from a man.

In 1994, I came across the work of Elizabeth Kubler Ross, who wrote the book, *On Death and Dying - What the Dying Have to Teach Doctors, Nurses, Clergy and Their Own Families*. In the 1970s,[20] she worked tirelessly to champion the beginnings of Hospice in this country. Through research and conducting interviews with hundreds of people who were at the end of their lives, Ross was able to identify five different stages that most terminal people go through:

1. Denial
2. Anger
3. Bargaining
4. Depression
5. Acceptance

Ross's work challenged the work of traditional clinical approaches to death and dying, as she believed that people deserved to be treated with compassion and caring.

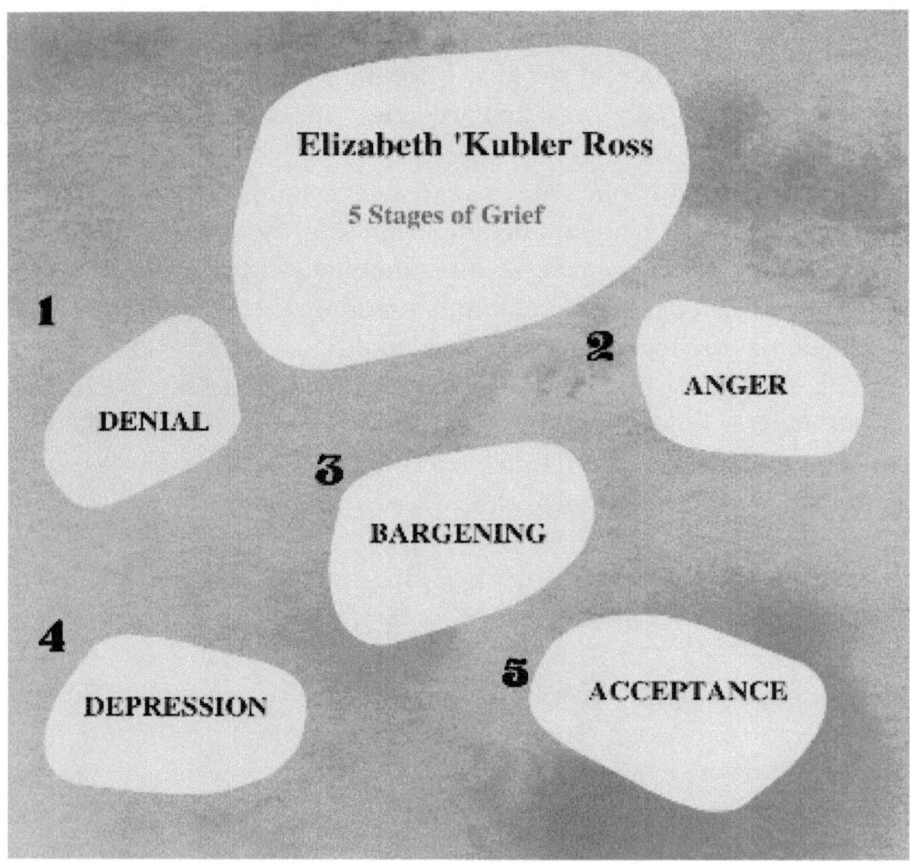

Although Ross worked with people who were terminally ill, like most humans, I have gone through the grieving stages with other losses during my lifetime. I could have stayed in that downward spiral after Karen transitioned, but knowing about the five stages, I was better able to understand my grief over Karen's death.

I understand now the greatest gift Karen gave me was the ability to receive *and* give love unconditionally to multiple friends. I will be eternally grateful for her friendship and for God putting her in my life. Even through her death, I learned great lessons.

I experienced other types of grief in my life. For example, I worked as the program director in an adult daycare in 2003. When my core values of integrity, honesty, and compassion no longer aligned with the company policies, I resigned–but not without regrets. I grieved the loss of that job because I missed the clients I worked with. This time, however, I could quickly see how being in that position had prepared me for my future leadership roles.

We sometimes need to part ways with a job or a friend because we have grown or outgrown the situation and want different things out of life. It doesn't mean it is anyone's fault, necessarily; it is just time to move on. Professional athletes know their careers will eventually come to an end. They grieve it still, and this change requires them to find a different position in their sport or find a different way to spend their days.

After we actively spend nearly two decades or so years raising each of our children, they go out on their own. Suddenly, we are left to ourselves, becoming empty nesters, sometimes realizing we don't know who we are as a person; we have lost ourselves, and we need to grieve the loss of our former life.

Renewed Thoughts of Reiki

I was watching a movie about a family's nervousness about their mother's upcoming surgery. It brought back the memory of Karen's hospital stay the night before her surgery and the reiki treatment she had. I dug around in the pile of papers I had stuck in a drawer until I found the woman's name who encouraged me to put my hands on Karen's knees. Her name was Lisa.

I began to have reiki treatments myself from Lisa regularly. It helped me tremendously. The ache in my heart over my loss of Karen, which had dissipated over time, was gradually replaced with acceptance and deep gratitude for the experiences. This convinced me to do the training myself, and I have now been a reiki master for over twenty-five years, helping myself, my family, and clients with this profound healing modality.

So, you may ask, what is reiki? The word reiki is composed of two Japanese words: *rei*, which means "God's Wisdom or the Higher Power" and *ki*, which is "life force energy".[21]

What reiki is *not:* a replacement for treatment by a licensed medical professional. Instead, reiki is a simple, natural, safe method of spiritual healing and self-improvement that anyone can use.

This modality has been effective in helping virtually every known illness and always creates a beneficial effect. It also works in conjunction with all other medical or therapeutic techniques to relieve side effects and promote recovery. It is a technique for stress reduction and relaxation. If one's energy is low, one is more likely to get sick, so the movement of energy and raising one's energy promotes healing. Reiki is administered by laying on hands and is based on the idea that an unseen energy flows through us.

Reiki allows the muscles to relax, which increases the blood flow to the areas that it is being administered. Scientists will tell you this, indeed, quickens the healing process. Reiki is being used in over eight hundred hospital settings nationwide as a valid modality. A treatment feels like there is wonderful energy flowing through and around you. Reiki treats the whole person, including body, emotions, mind, and spirit, creating many beneficial effects, including relaxation and feelings of peace, security, and well-being.

Many have reported miraculous results, but like any treatment, it depends on the individual and the circumstances. For example, during Karen's cancer treatments, reiki helped her to manage her present state better. No matter what, energy is advantageous for healing problems, including the release of anger, fear and worry, sadness, and many other unhealthy feelings. And over time, like for me, the client begins to have a sense of self-worth and confidence.

Things I Have Learned

The order in which we process the five steps of grief isn't carved in stone, and sometimes we revisit one or two of the stages over again. Grief and sadness can have many layers, just like an onion that needs to be peeled back to get to the core.

Even though I had worked on an issue or trauma and felt relief, sometimes it resurfaced again sometime later. My initial thought was,

I dealt with that already; why is it here again? But upon further consideration, I realized through reiki the emotion was not nearly as strong as before, and my emotional discomfort didn't last as long. I was able to give myself kudos for doing the work, and you can too.

Some Actions to Consider Taking to Help You Work through Your Grief

- Pick up a past interest or hobby or start something new.
- Offer your time doing service work.
- Develop or deepen your spiritual or religious beliefs.
- Join a grief support group.
- Consider trying alternative healing modalities like reiki, foot-zoning, cranial fascial massage, or others that have proven to have remarkable benefits in processing grief in the mind, emotions, and body.
- Be compassionate. Not one person's grief looks exactly like another's. Your grief timeline-and even what it looks like-is uniquely your own.

CHAPTER TWELVE

Embrace Your Inner Child

Hold the hand of the child that lives in your soul.
For this child, nothing is impossible.
—*Paulo Coelho*

Meeting your inner child can heal your past, present, and future self. In your past resides memories of any traumas that may still linger in the shadows of the mind. This is normal for every human who's been around the block a time or two. Still, it is possible to observe life more fully and consciously in the present.

What if I were to tell you there is a simple process to become thoroughly acquainted with your younger self, commonly referred to as your inner child? Would you be interested? If we can see things through our child's eye, we have the power to re-parent our younger selves and show them they are loved and precious–even if that was not what their experiences taught them. Something significant happens when we can see our child's perspective about a hurtful or traumatic event.

When we become adults, our reasoning capabilities mature. Yet on some level, the memories of relationships or events from childhood remain in a child's perspective, frozen in time at the age we were when the trauma occurred.

Doing inner-child work helps us to recognize how our behaviors as an adult can originate from childhood experiences. It can then allow us to focus and address unmet needs we didn't get from our parents while growing up.

When attending the John Bradshaw workshop, confronting my dad during the meditation, and working with my inner child, somehow, I felt lighter. Since then, I have combined automatic writing, which I will discuss in depth later in this chapter, with other tools to work with my younger self.

After my marriage to John, I went to my friend, Jackie, for a massage when she showed me a flyer about a series of workshops by a renowned author to become a certified spiritual counselor. This was intriguing to me because several of my clients had come to me for a reiki session due to a spiritual crisis, and I had the desire to help further. But the course was scheduled to start the next day in Phoenix, Arizona!

Jackie's eyes lit up as she told me about some of the experiences she had been having while "working with her angels when giving reiki sessions, which was a new process for her." Her enthusiasm was contagious. I didn't understand that the concept of working with my angels meant calling on them for help, just as I would call for God's help. I made a hurried trip out to the Southwest Airlines reservation center where I was employed, logged onto the computer, and snagged the last two seats. Somehow, I knew my life would change radically; I had no clue just how much.

The workshop's format was designed to introduce different types of healing methods.

A whole new world of healing modalities opened to me that would complement my work. It was amazing. I began thinking about how I would implement some things for my clients.

The instructor taught us how to communicate with another person's higher self (either still living or with someone who had passed on), using a technique called automatic writing.[22] We were instructed to select someone we wanted to speak to. The whole room went quiet as people began the process.

I was skeptical at first that I would have anyone come through, but I was open to giving it a try. I did *not* expect the person who came through to chat with me. Within moments, I knew it was my grandfather, my dad's father, Oliver.

The first thing he said was, "*What's with all of those damned totes?*"

I knew exactly what my grandpa was referring to with his comment. I almost burst out loud with laughter. It just so happened that after both my grandparents had passed, I was able to take many rocks they had gathered through the years as rockhounds. The rocks held a special place in my heart because I had been going with them beginning at age five.

I could still smell the aroma of the sagebrush while searching for red jasper or topaz crystals in the deserts of Utah. A smile came to my face when I pictured my short, stocky grandma wearing jeans, revealing her bowed legs, a plaid shirt, and a hat, bent over, looking for newfound treasures. Grandpa was wearing a safari hat, contently working alongside her.

The rocks had been placed in a three-tiered fashion around what we called the back porch, making a fabulous rock garden that included petrified wood pieces and large agates, among other kinds. A large thirteen-and-a-half-pound quartz crystal now adorns the hearth of my fireplace, holding space for a reiki grid. I brought home several dozen or so rocks and recreated a fantastic display in my yard.

At one point, John and I moved to California, but sadly many of my treasured rocks got broken in the move. When we moved again, I bought a bunch of plastic totes to protect them from more breakage.

During our conversation, Grandpa reminded me of a particular trip to Topaz Mountain we had taken before Utah officially named topaz as the state gem. He had been on the committee to lobby for the legislation to have topaz named as the Utah state gemstone. Then, Grandpa told me he thought I had done an excellent job with my children and he loved me. The whole experience of speaking with my grandfather was very profound.

When I returned home after my training, one of my good friends looked at me and asked, "Who are you, and what did you do with my friend?" All I could do was acknowledge his observation with a huge grin on my face. I had indeed come home to a different person. I retained valuable new awarenesses and skills I knew I could use to help people along their journey and continue on mine.

Using a Proxy to Communicate

With determination to continue what I had started at the workshop taught by John Bradshaw, I sat down in my overstuffed chair to talk to my younger self. I lovingly placed my new fuzzy stuffed bear to be used as my proxy in a chair across from me and began our healing session via pen and paper.

During our first conversation, holding the pen in my dominant hand, representing my adult self, I asked her what she wanted to be called.

She replied, "Well, Julie Ann, of course!" via my non-dominant hand.

I then asked her what she needed. During the back-and-forth conversation, we established her need for love and acceptance that she had not received as a young girl. I listened to her describe the horror she felt at age eight when Dad made such a spectacle at the pool at Black Rock and shamed and humiliated her. I reassured her I loved her and would always be there for her.

When I completed the process, I felt a peace in my heart I hadn't known before. I promised Julie Ann we would often speak, which we have done.

After working with Julie Ann, I discovered it was and continues to be a great way to feel connected to my inner child.

Doing inner-child work and using a proxy helps bring natural compassion and an understanding that you have wounds that still need to be healed, usually from your childhood. Using automatic writing to speak to your wounded younger self can give you the love and acceptance you didn't receive as a child, but you can now offer yourself. So, let's get into how to utilize this tool to its total capacity when using the technique of automatic writing.

The Technique

1. Allow yourself to be open-minded.
2. Find a place where you won't be disturbed or distracted.
3. Take a moment to clear your mind. Listen to calming music if desired.

4. Inhale deeply, hold your breath for the count of four, and exhale to the count of six. Repeat three times.

5. Invite your younger self to have a conversation with you. Be mindful that your inner child may be resistive because there may be mistrust that an adult would even take the time to listen.

6. Tell your inner self it is safe to express themselves and reassure them that you *want* to hear what they say. Repeat the breathwork if needed to alleviate any resistance.

7. Using your dominant hand, ask your child what name they want to be called.

8. Placing a pen in your dominant hand and writing down a question to your younger self, ask them what they need or want to tell you. Switch the pen to your other hand and wait for the answer. Try not to second-guess yourself. It will come from your inner child, who is wise and all-knowing. Allow the solution to flow through.

9. Continue the conversation until you feel complete in the process.

10. End the session by expressing gratitude to your child for the trust and willingness to participate in the exercise.

I was surprised and pleased as my letter became a longer back-and-forth conversation over time. When I completed the process, I felt peace in my heart for my progress in connecting to my inner child once again. I received some beautiful insights, provided genuine listening and caring to her, and I promised her we would spend time together playing and allowing ourselves to be silly.

Before Karen passed, we used this "conversation" tool often with great success in working through many traumas from our respective childhoods. We were able to have even deeper confidence to cut loose and play more often. (If that was even possible, since I think we had gotten quite good at cutting loose.)

In Summary

I didn't share about speaking to my grandfather just to tell you I was communicating with a dead person, but to show how powerful and significant automatic writing can be. Using the technique also deepened the relationship with Julie Ann and with myself, and that healing carried out into other relationships. That will not only help you heal the past but can help you in the present stand up for yourself once and for all.

You can find a link on my website for a PDF for the steps to take you through a healing session using automatic writing. http://madisonfrederick.com/.

CHAPTER THIRTEEN

My Illusion of My Birth Mother

Absence is a house so vast that inside you will pass
through its walls and hang pictures in the air.
—Pablo Neruda

Abandonment is a simple word with several emotional connotations: rejection, desertion, neglect, withdrawal, and betrayal. Experiencing the fallout from these emotions can leave a hole in the bucket we call life. If these holes are left unattended, they can create havoc and drain us completely dry.

Even in early childhood, abandonment issues can carry on into adulthood and, if not addressed, can cause lingering, tragic effects in our current relationships. I have felt abandoned in close relationships with friends in addition to my family. Healing begins when you are willing to tell yourself the truth.

My birth parents divorced when I was three years old. That's when my mother, Margaret, left. My grandma told me Margaret had randomly visited me for a little while, but she stopped coming by to see me when I was four. I didn't give it much thought until things went sideways with my new stepmom.

Grandma had shown me a picture of Margaret, and I thought she looked like Judy Garland. When I got upset or angry as a kid, which happened quite often, I hid under my dressing table and fantasized Margaret would somehow hear my tears and rescue me. My heart ached to connect with my mother, to feel loved and cherished.

In the afternoon of my eighteenth birthday, out of the blue, I received a phone call from Granny, Margaret's mother. She invited me to come to dinner. I hadn't heard from her in about fourteen years.

During the phone call, Granny made it very clear how she had antic-ipated reaching out to me on that exact day for a long time. "I prom-ised your dad on your eighteenth birthday I would be calling you, but I would stay away from you so as not to confuse you. I threatened him that he better not be telling you untruths about Granddad and me. And here I am!" she robustly declared.

I had received a few birthday cards from Granny through the years, so I agreed to go to dinner at their place out of curiosity. If you remem-ber from a few chapters ago, at eighteen years old, I had just gotten engaged to Ron the day before, so I insisted on bringing him along.

On our drive to the apartment, I began to feel apprehensive, not knowing what to expect. Old fears from childhood started rearing up inside my body. *Will I be welcomed? How will the evening go? I have no idea what I will talk about. I wonder if I will be shown pictures of Margaret or receive any news about her or her life.*

When we arrived, I hesitantly rang the doorbell. Granny answered the door with excitement displayed across her entire face. This near stranger flung her arms wide open, ready to embrace me.

I wasn't sure how to respond and kept my arms held stiffly at my sides. Her grip was gentle despite my resistance to being embraced by someone I didn't know as she drew me inside the apartment. She was a thin woman with short, silver-gray hair. Her curls framed her face, and she wore tan, polyester pants with an orange and brown print blouse.

Sitting in a big, overstuffed green chair across the room was Grandad. He had silver-rimmed glasses and was wearing a big, wel-coming smile on his face as well. From what I could tell, he was a tall man, confirmed when he rose. Grandad extended his hand and enthusiastically shook mine.

I noticed someone sitting on the sofa next to Grandad's chair. She looked vaguely familiar to me, like the woman in the one picture I had been shown of my birth mother when I was five or six.

Could this be Margaret? I wondered. She was wearing a pink sweater and dark pants with her hands folded tightly in her lap. Margaret stayed seated and looked as nervous as I felt. Granny mentioned Margaret just "happened" to come for a visit, but it seemed this meeting was pre-planned. I didn't buy any of it!

Using short sentences, I answered their questions but didn't ask many of my own. Annoyed at both of them, I felt highly uncomfortable despite Ron being there.

I don't remember all of the dinner conversations. However, I remember being confused about how I should feel. I struggled to come up with anything to say. I couldn't keep my thoughts from drifting back to the "surprise" appearance of my birth mother. I was throwing around tons of questions of my own in my head.

Should I be grateful Margaret is here? Should I be angry because she has not explained why she has never returned to see me all this time? I glanced over at her and then quickly went away. *Where have you been all this time, Margaret?* I simply didn't know what to think.

I glanced at the clock on the wall and calculated how many more minutes we should stay so I didn't appear rude. I felt all the dining room walls closing in and around me. I could not wait to get out of there.

As soon as we got in my car, I told Ron, "I don't trust Margaret."

"I don't think I would either," he answered with a soft chuckle. After that night, I did not reach out to any of them and focused on my upcoming marriage and the new life I would have some time in the near future away from Utah.

Ron was gone on another long deployment; we had been living in California for about two and a half years after being ambushed by Granny and Margaret. I was lonely and thinking about Margaret. I decided I should try to give her a second chance. Maybe there was an explanation as to why she had abandoned me. I thought about how my young daughter deserved to have an opportunity to have a relationship with her grandmother. So, I sent Margaret a letter, and we began corresponding. I slowly embraced her back into my life. After about six months of writing letters back and forth, she flew to California for a short visit.

During her stay, Margaret told me she had quit coming to visit me when I was four years old because my dad and grandma made it too difficult for her to see me. She said she was always told it wouldn't be a convenient time when she did try. I wanted to believe Margaret's explanation, yet always on the tip of my tongue, the burning question went unsaid: *but why did you abandon me in the first place?* I was too frightened to ask. I rationalized that she *was* in my life now, and I didn't want to rock the boat.

Then, as if she read my mind, she said, "I never abandoned you!" With a sad voice, she again repeated, "I never abandoned you because I have always loved you."

I just looked at her. *Always loved me? Really? How would I ever have any way of knowing that?* That day I successfully stuffed my feelings down my throat like I always did.

Margaret and I continued to write letters back and forth, and I saw her usually twice a year when we traveled to Salt Lake City for a visit. Each time it became more and more difficult. I wanted to tell Margaret how much she had hurt me and how I wasn't buying her reasoning. Her rationale didn't make any sense. Ever since I was a little girl, she had abandoned me in my mind. However, I couldn't level with her for fear of being left with nothing. Again.

Margaret disappeared from my life once more two years later. I'm not sure what happened; she just quit answering my letters. By then, Ron was deployed on another Westpac cruise. In November of 1977, my little girl and I flew to Salt Lake for a visit. We were only going to be in town for a week.

It had been two years since the last time I had any contact with Margaret. I decided to call her, hoping we could bury the hatchet and try again. I told Margaret how much I had missed her, and I was excited to get together. I breathed a sigh of relief when she agreed to see me. We made plans to go to lunch and then go shopping the next day.

When I called Margaret that morning to confirm the pick-up time, she told me she would have to cancel because she needed to spend time with Mary, one of her close friends. Mary was having some kind of personal crisis, and Margaret told me she was obligated in her words to be there for her.

"Why don't we all go together?" I suggested. "It may help Mary get her mind off what is going on with her."

During that conversation, Margaret admitted to me her friend Mary didn't even know I existed, and she couldn't have me come because she didn't know what she would say to explain why she hadn't told Mary about me.

Shocked and silent, I thought, *I've heard all about Mary, so why won't Margaret tell her about me?* I knew Margaret had been friends with Mary for over twenty years, but she had never mentioned me during that time.

How could she choose Mary over me? It is like when my stepmom laughed at me when her friend Irma made fun of my name. She had chosen her friendship with her over my feelings! I told myself that she'd probably been lying to me about loving me. I was so pissed that I couldn't say anything else, so I hung up on her. I would never give her another chance; I was done with her!

When I was thirty-two, we returned to Utah in 1984 and purchased a house. We wanted to get established before Ron retired from the military. I was excited to be around my sweet, sweet grandma again. I wanted to also reconnect with Granny and Grandad. During a visit with them, I ran into Margaret, unexpectedly this time. She was cordial and suggested we meet for coffee in two days at a newly opened coffee house.

It is located right across the street from Liberty Park, one of my favorite places in all of Salt Lake Valley, partly because the Tracy Aviary is located right inside the park. I also loved spending time around the numerous trees because I am fascinated with tree knots. There were plenty of unusual ones.

It was comforting and a joy for me to discover that both Margaret and I had a deep love of birds. My favorite is the snowy owl, also known as the polar owl, and hers was a barn owl, both of which we enjoyed visiting during our walk-throughs in the aviary. One day, Margaret gave me a small wooden carving of a snowy owl, which I named Sydney. I treasured the gift.

Over the next eight years, we spent more and more time together, going to lunch, shopping, or having coffee. However, I was still stifling my feelings. I could not use my voice and come clean about how I truly felt about the many times she had abandoned me throughout the years. One of my biggest hurts was not just her choice to spend time with Mary instead of me–it had more to do with emotional abandonment. I was still crushed because she had kept me a secret from those closest to her.

My children and I were invited to Margaret's extended family gatherings. Margaret had five siblings, and they all had many children, so I got acquainted with many of my cousins. It was so much fun listening to all the stories about my birth mother's antics with her two sisters. It was a dream come true for me to be around a huge, loving family.

Margaret even supported me during my divorce from Ron, and I will never forget how she paid for the rehearsal dinner when I married my soulmate John in 1990. It was such a tender gesture, and for that and a hundred different reasons, I felt like she had indeed become family.

I was struggling with finding harmony with my new little family. Between my new husband and my twelve-year-old son, I always felt caught in the middle of any disagreement they had with each other. I started seeing a therapist and learned that it often happens when adjusting to a new family dynamic.

I had been in therapy for about six months when my mental health took a nosedive. I also learned that this is common when any trauma is acknowledged and worked on in a person's life. That was comforting, but I was in so much pain and struggling to function daily. My life got very dark, and I started thinking about how I could end it all. I even came up with a plan.

My therapist gently invited me to go to a residential treatment facility, as he put it, "to take a little break from the tension at home." I accepted the offer and checked myself in. I was prescribed medication and the staff helped me work through some things while I was there. I did a lot of journaling, and through that process, I realized it was time for me to put my big girl panties on and level with Margaret.

I wrote Margaret a letter, and on the day I was to be discharged, I gave it to her to read during her visit. I watched her face for any indication of her reaction. I didn't have to wait very long. She'd only read a page when her coloring went from pale white to beet red. Margaret crumpled the letter and threw it at me.

She sneered. "I told you I didn't abandon you, and *YOU* told me you understood." She looked me straight in the eye and declared, "I have put my guard down for you four times now," she bellowed, "and I am not doing it again!" And with that, she turned on her heel and stomped out of the room.

Margaret and I never spoke again.

The Abyss of Motherly Affection

Twenty years later, John stumbled onto Margaret's obituary. I was not mentioned as her daughter, not even as a footnote. Despite all I had worked on, it broke my heart once again to see myself abandoned, even in her death. Here's the thing: relationships are essential. What we do and who we come to care for has a ripple. I learned from Margaret some valuable lessons about what *not* to do to others. In my own way, I was grateful for the time and the walks we did have with each other before she left my life again. I am also so grateful for the loving support of my husband, John, who held my heart in his hands after reading the notice of Margaret's death. He helped me to realize what was permanent and what was not.

Five years after Margaret passed, I wrote a second letter to her. I lit a white, unscented candle and defused a blend of essential oils: peppermint, the oil for uplifting, and wild orange, to bring in the abundance of joy. I told her that I realized I had transferred my hurt and frustration onto her when I wrote that letter while in the treatment center. I realized I wanted to punish her, so she would feel all of the pain I had felt all those years. I told her I wasn't proud of any of that.

I owned my piece of the past situation's turmoil. I told her how sorry I was and that I loved her. I burned the letter with the intent to release any residual toxic energy that might have been left. I also went to the cemetery where she was laid to rest, and in a special, respectful ceremony, I buried near Margaret's headstone a healing quartz crystal along with Sydney. This snowy owl figurine had significance to both of us.

I still go to Liberty Park often, and that coffee shop is now one of my and John's favorites. I am at peace now, although I often miss Margaret and think of her often. I'd like to believe that she's on her beautiful journey on the other side, and that sometime we will meet and laugh about our stubborn behavior.

Things I Have Learned

Up until I was in my late thirties, I had never entirely been able to use my voice for several reasons. Parts of me were afraid of being abandoned again, and the other fear was not being heard. I had many holes in my bucket called life, which created havoc. Slowly I began to acknowledge that I needed and deserved to speak up. I permitted myself to speak my truth. Slowly, one by one, I began to patch and heal the holes in my bucket.

As much as I wanted to be fully healed, if I had tried to face the hurdle of getting past each abandonment issue all at one time, it would have been too much for me to take on. It needed to be disassembled, brick by brick, person by person.

I was in my fifties before I was genuinely able to take an honest look and take *full* responsibility for myself and my actions regarding my birth mother. It was necessary to acknowledge my piece in the breakdown of the relationship with Margaret, piece by piece.

For one thing, I realized I hadn't considered that my birth mother may just not have been ready to see me, and I had taken it all too personally. It probably didn't have anything to do with me. At least, in the beginning, it likely had nothing to do with me at all and everything to do with her own difficulties she was facing.

I certainly experienced a rough time growing up with my narcissistic father. Indeed, being in a relationship with him and birthing his child could not have been easy for her. And I'll never know whether something happened to her at age four, or if it was the pain of having to leave me when I was four. We are all complex characters on an essential and challenging journey.

All the years I spent blaming and justifying my anger at Margaret robbed me of a feeling of *peace*. I finally did the work, and then I could disassemble the web of my silence. I filled my holes with self-love instead of blame or shame. I now feel whole and complete after letting go of all of the toxic energy from the entire situation with Margaret.

Take Some Time to Consider These Questions about Abandonment and Boundaries

Have you ever felt abandoned by a parent? A lover? A spouse? A best friend?

- Have you ever compartmentalized any areas in your life to avoid looking at them?
- Where, and in what relationships have you not used your voice?
- What are the reasons for not doing so?
- Is it time to level with someone and use your voice and speak your truth?

For help with finding your voice, contact me at: https://www.madisonfrederick.com.

CHAPTER FOURTEEN

Forgiving Narcissism . . . and Other Human Frailties

To forgive is to set a prisoner free and discover that the prisoner was you.
—Lewis B. Smedes

I have shared with you throughout this book that my healing journey has taken me down a path with many forks on the road that helped me figure things out. Writing this book was very cathartic for me. When I began this manuscript, it looked very different than it does now. I, like many others, have found that the first draft was written for myself. And then I wrote it for the reader. From the beginning, what became blatantly clear to me was that the first person I needed to forgive in order to move on was me.

While I was nearing the completion of the book, I recognized that my dad had a backstory that shaped his life and choices. Dad was a human who made human mistakes. Even though it was excruciating, and I certainly disagree with his actions, I learned to be compassionate toward him. It allowed me to remember some of the good memories I can now hold in my heart.

I do not discount my dad's unhealthiness and dysfunctional behaviors or my acting out the learned behaviors I had put into practice before I knew better. We are all born with a higher purpose to fulfill in our lifetime. We are given opportunities to learn from our mistakes and missteps. I also believe I needed to endure all the traumas to get to the other side so I could author this book with the purpose in mind of helping others.

Because of all the hate in our hearts, we only focus on our pain, and our memories become cloudy. I don't remember any happy moments from my early childhood, but a few came to mind. I began remembering things my dad did that were kind.

Before my dad and I moved out of my grandma's house at age five, I thought of myself as Daddy's little princess. I remember Dad arriving home late at night after his shift at a local television station. I pretended to be asleep with my head buried under the covers. Our private party began when he turned on the record player. As the record spun around, playing the song, "The Green Door" by Jim Lowe, I gently slipped from the bed onto the floor. Dad took my hand so we could dance. I begged, "Play it one more time, please."

"Just once more, and then you must go to sleep," he answered.

It always made me feel like I *was* his little princess. It was a particular time for me, and I truly felt loved in those moments.

Another time Dad arrived home early and surprised me so we could go to the Utah State fair. Before leaving the house, we made our favorite sandwich, a hot dog with mustard. Dad split the dogs in two, and I got to put the mustard on the bread. My favorite part of the fair was looking at the livestock. These memories remind me that it wasn't all bad; he did love me.

My mom made me a pixie haircut. I thought it made me look like a boy. Plus, she bought a romper and demanded I wear it. I felt humiliated.

Dad led me into the gift shop. He wanted to buy me a fishing pole to teach me how to fish. I was confused by his kindness until he told me he thought it would take my mind off the short haircut. Once again, I felt like a protected princess.

After I learned about the *ho'oponopono* prayer, I was able to open my heart even further and begin the process of forgiving myself on a deeper level. One prayer at a time, I started letting go of the animosity I had lived with regarding my dad's narcissism.

The ho'oponopono prayer is a beautiful Hawaiian way of teaching forgiveness.[23] While saying it, you can recall a particular relationship to which you want to bring forth healing and forgiveness. Repeat each line three times:

"I'm sorry; please forgive me; thank you, I love you."

Just as I have been able to do with family members, I can now remember there *are* happy memories to hold in my heart. You also can have the same results.

CHAPTER FIFTEEN

The No Contact Clause

What we once enjoyed and deeply loved we can never lose,
For all that we love deeply becomes a part of us.
—Helen Keller

bandonment happens when a person lets go of any responsibility and ownership of something. On the other hand, *estrangement* is when a person is alienated or separated from a relationship. Sometimes there is even hostility involved.[24]

In the aftermath of the estrangement with my son, I asked myself if there was something I could have done differently to prevent it from happening. And I wondered how I was going to make it through my loss. I did find answers for myself to both of these questions, and I will share my thoughts in this chapter.

I came to understand that my birth mother, Margaret, had abandoned me repeatedly, especially after I was an adult. There were gaps between the years we were in contact, but the times we connected and talked were a cornucopia of emotions for me: fun, pain, and confusion, leaving me with an itch I could never seem to scratch.

Over fifty-two-years, Margaret had been in and out of my life four times. The final time, when we went our separate ways in 1994, she decided to create an estrangement in our relationship because of the letter I had written while in the treatment center.

I was bitter and angry regarding Margaret until choosing to do my healing work over these past three decades. In writing this book, working with my clients and some of their very real abandonment issues, as well as through some of my own experiences regarding abandonment and estrangement, I realized there are multiple and varied situations in which both abandonment and estrangement can play out.

They all have lasting consequences in relationships. In gathering the stories of clients and others I have interviewed, I have witnessed firsthand the struggle of balancing the emotions that have ebbed and flowed through their veins.

After I received the "email bombshell" from my son with the no contact clause, I was astonished to learn there were far too many of us aboard the *USS Estrangement*, floating in an ocean of guilt and shame, humiliation, despair, anger, and sadness—waiting for the life raft of reconciliation with our loved ones.

What Defines Guilt and Shame?

From my experience, I have felt *guilty* when I did or thought I did something wrong, such as the time I ate all of the candy in the gift shop in the hospital as a candy striper and didn't pay for it.

Shame is when you believe you are wrong, and then tell yourself that whatever the situation is, it's all your fault. An example is when I tried to justify myself when my granddaughter found the Tylenol and I asked my son what the big deal was. And then realized I had messed up with my comment.

When someone becomes estranged from their child, the burning questions seared in mind can become: *What are my friends and relatives going to think of my parenting abilities? Will they believe the separation is my fault? What will my religious community think of me?* In a world where society often determines who is at fault, blame and shame feel significant when an adult child cuts the parent(s) out of their lives. And even if you are the one walking away, there is an aftermath of emotions.

I replayed the memories of the numerous times I had been abandoned and had taken the victim's stance myself. That is, until I started my quest for a healthier life after divorcing Ron. There can come a time when a parent *can* stop the shame and intense self-blame, choosing to take responsibility for their part in the relationship and perhaps whatever unhealthy contributions they have made.

Over the last several years with my clients, I have watched many struggles to understand what happened in their estranged relationships. They are primarily plagued with the question of why? Often, they feel they are not to blame–it's the other person's fault that the rift began. At least at first. I know I blamed others for many years.

An article by columnist David Brooks in the *New York Times*[25] states at least twenty-seven percent of Americans are estranged from a member of their own family. When you think about it, that's a large percentage of the population! And about forty percent of Americans have experienced estrangement at some point. The most common form is between adult children and one or both parents—a cut usually initiated by the child.

I have discovered that estrangement is a complex issue with as many opinions and variables as possible in different life situations for an estrangement to occur.

Here are just a few:

- There are times when an adult child or parent has been influenced by someone or something else. It could be that an ex-spouse, brother-in-law, daughter-in-law, mother-in-law, or a chemical addiction is in play.
- It can be dramatic and confusing. My client Beth stated, "I've agonized, cried, and apologized, even though I don't know what to apologize for! I don't understand why this has happened. I've done nothing wrong."
- It can be infuriating or even terrifying. Jamal, another client, cited, "Ever since my daughter got married, my son-in-law has turned her against us, and she won't answer her phone or my emails."
- It can feel helpless and humiliating. "After my divorce, my ex-husband told my son lies, turning him against me," my friend Mary shared as she hung her head down. "Several years later, I went to his graduation from army boot camp. He spotted me, turned, and walked in the other direction, avoiding me," she added with tears in her eyes.

Not all estrangements are between a parent and a child. A client I recently worked with was a woman who hadn't seen or had any contact with her cousins for over twenty years, partly due to geographical distances and partly because her aunt didn't want her children to have contact with her. It didn't keep the situation from being any less painful for her.

Estrangement hurts deeply. It can also be an important wake-up call. Taking a deep and honest inventory of my past behaviors with my children was paramount for my personal growth. I had used justification when I couldn't take responsibility for my words or actions, which, justifiably for my son, became the ultimate reason he cut me out of his life—and why he sent me that infamous email in the first place.

Was I a perfect parent? No, I wasn't. But I finally understood that I did the best I could with the tools I had *at the time.* I have delved deeply into psychology and behavioral observation. I now understand how my dad and stepmother, as well as my birth mother, Margaret, modeled the only parenting skills I learned. It was all I knew.

Despite taking on that accountability, I have experienced many emotions since becoming estranged from my son and his family. I have felt deep sadness, anger, fear of missing out (FOMO), and jealousy of others' relationships with their children and grandchildren. As I mentioned, I even struggled with severe depression in the past. While I am grateful that I have learned excellent skills in emotional healing, release, and overcoming skills, I admit my heart still aches to have contact with my son's family and especially my grandchildren again.

If you are working on feelings of abandonment and are experiencing estrangement from any of your meaningful relationships, it's important to note a couple of things:

1. If you were the one who cut off the relationship, conduct an inventory of the reasons for the split. Did you do it based on safety or a vendetta? If you were choosing healthier behavior patterns, lifestyles, and relationships, you might have had substantial reasons for the separation. Keep in mind that people grow and change, just as you do. What was necessary then, however, might

no longer be so, as was shown in the statistics quoted in Brooks'
column.

2. Whether or not you were responsible for the no contact clause
   or if it was someone else's doing, keep in mind that you did the
   best you knew how. It is essential to realize this point for yourself.
   This principle is *key* to giving yourself compassion in your case
   and moving on in your life the best way you can now. If you can
   learn from the situation, you might not need to experience such
   a wake-up call in the future, having more extraordinary skill sets
   than before.

Parent/Child Dynamics Have Changed

Adult children today often don't find the need to hang out with their
parents regularly. While some do, many have developed a new and different obligation to their parents and siblings. Sometimes this involves
"checking in," and other times involves little to no participation.

Using Emotional Freedom Technique or "Tapping"

In addition to talk therapy, I also used the Emotional Freedom
Technique (EFT) tapping to navigate all of the emotions that came up
around my estrangement. It is a simple technique that can be used to
work on the subconscious wiring of the brain. It helps to reduce stress
and anxiety.

EFT involves tapping, using your fingers on specific points on the
body, primarily on the head and face in a particular sequence. It
helps deactivate any emotional response that can sometimes appear
as physical and emotional pain that we may be experiencing due to
a situation or memory of a past event. Using this process, I focused
on the estrangement with my son while tapping on specific points of
the body, and therefore changing the stimulus and response to it in
mind and body.

Steps I Took to Strengthen Myself in My Estrangement

- I took responsibility for the ways I contributed to the situation.
- In prayer and meditation, I slowly began to forgive myself.
- I used essential oils to ease anxiety and help with forgiveness.
- I continued using EFT tapping.
- I began to feel immense compassion for everyone involved.
- I recognized I needed to develop my own identity outside of being a mother.
- I wrote my first letter to my son, getting all of my anger out on paper, after which I burned it, with the intention of letting go of any lingering emotion that didn't serve either of us.
- Two years later, I wrote a second letter and mailed it to my son. Going through and sending it was one of the most challenging and liberating things I have ever done.
- I prayed to God to remove any expectations I had for any outcome with mailing the letter.
- In the letter, I made amends for the ways in which I was wrong.

Five years after Margaret had passed, I learned how to do a technique called The Butterfly Code™ created by Michael Blackstone of Mentor International, Inc. The code is a process in which a declaration is written, calling on your Higher Power for the best possible outcome and a resolution of feelings like hurt, frustration, and abandonment.

I took myself through the process of writing a Butterfly Code in regards to Margaret. In addition to making the declaration, I meditated and lit a white, unscented candle and defused a powerful blend of essential oils called Adaptiv® while expressing gratitude for the technique of The Butterfly Code™, for Michael's work, and for the powerful lessons I'd been given.

You can try one or all of these, which might assist you on your journey. In working with clients, I have seen important patterns at play, and recognize there are vital actions you can take that will help you on your journey.

Actions You Can Take to Strengthen Yourself

- Recognize how important it is to look after yourself and honor those still in your life.
- Write down the positive things you did in your relationship, no matter how trivial they seem. When you make your list, there is an opportunity to see all of the good choices in black and white. Once again, keep in mind you did the best with the tools you had at the time.
- Find a therapist who specializes in family trauma. Be open to feedback and processes. Get the help you need for as long as you may need it.
- Learn to have deep compassion for yourself.
- Find a Facebook group for support. Whether public or private, there are many available, with hundreds of active members. Here are a few that helped me:
  o Estranged Mothers Support Group
  o Dr. Joshua Coleman Parent/Grand-parent Estrangement Support Group
  o Group Family Estrangement Support Group

Things to Think About

When I looked deeply at my situation, I could finally see some definite areas I could have done differently, more effectively, and in a healthier manner. But that was in hindsight. There are so many layers to each person's psyche that it can sometimes take years to uncover what makes us tick.

My stepbrother Randy and I were expected to stay home after school. We only saw our parents at dinnertime and on weekends. I didn't want that for my children when I became a parent. I was determined to have a different relationship with them than my parents.

In my mind, I saw what I thought a relationship "really should" be. I wanted to be there for my children while they were growing up. I *needed* to be a friend to my children when they grew up. My "need" became an obsession. Behaving like a helicopter parent and grandparent was also contributing to my son's decision to go his separate way. I had developed a codependency mindset because of my deep fear of being alone.

Now that I have moved beyond those unhealthy behaviors, my heart remains loving, conscious, and mindful. My husband and I carefully and considerately send our grandchildren cards on holidays and birthdays, wishing them well on such special occasions. We still honor my son's request and strive never to let anything except love now be our guide.

Lessons I Have Now Learned:

- It's okay never to stop caring. It's okay to love deeply and to grieve the loss.
- You can manage the pain in your heart much better when you practice self-care.
- You no longer have to allow your lives and your happiness to be in anyone else's control. For example, I'm choosing to live my best life with the time I have left.
- It's important to realize that your estranged loved one may come back, and perhaps they won't. That's not up to you–but your happiness and sanity are.

It has taken years to get where I am today and feel the peace I now feel. It can happen to you too. It's important to know this to take your next best step and live your best life!

> *The more a shared past there is in a relationship, the*
> *more present you need to be; otherwise, you will be*
> *forced to relive the past again and again.*
> *—Eckhart Tolle*

CHAPTER SIXTEEN

When Enough Is Never Enough

Breaking from food addiction is not just about losing weight.
It's about opening yourself to life.
—Laura Houssain

I s food fuel for you? Or do you use it as a crutch or protector against a certain feeling? Like millions of people, I have used food to soothe my anxieties for years in times of emotional pain. Whenever I was in psychological distress, I turned to food. This state is often referred to as HALT, an acronym for "hungry, angry, lonely, or tired."

Food addiction is very real for me, I assure you. I understand that declaring I am a food addict may sound drastic. Food addiction in some circles "does not exist." But as of May 2013, Binge Eating Disorder was added to the DSM (Diagnostic and Statistical Manual of Mental Disorders) as an actual eating disorder. That's not all. The Centers for Disease Control state that from 1999 through March 2020, in the US, the obesity prevalence increased from 30.5 percent to 41.9 percent of the population, and it's only increasing.

Body image, food, and weight go hand in hand. For me, things started at age six. My mom wanted to get mine and my brother's weights written in our baby books to track our growth. My brother was sent to retrieve the bathroom scales from the bathroom. After stepping off of the scales, Mom announced to the entire family that I was chubby and needed to lose weight. Feeling embarrassed, I was confused about what had just happened. No one had said anything about my weight before.

As an adult looking back, I remember Mom being a vain woman. I realized that weight and appearance were paramount in *her* life, like they were my father's, and had nothing to do with me. I watched as she took a can of Sego, a diet food replacement drink, to work almost every day for lunch. I was grateful her attention was on *her* weight most of the time instead of mine. However, she did continue to make snide remarks about my weight more times than I'd like to remember.

Someone once asked me when I first realized my overeating had become a problem. Looking back, I can see it was when I was twelve years old. I became aware of my food cravings getting out of hand when I was upset or stressed about something as a candy striper volunteering at the University of Utah Medical Center. Those were times I ate myself through all the sugar delights that filled the shelves in the gift shop.

I don't believe everyone who has weight to lose is addicted to food. Nor do I think everyone who gets drunk at a party is an alcoholic. I do know there are questions that you can ask yourself about your eating habits that may bring awareness if there is a possibility you have a problem.

1. Do you spend a significant amount of time thinking about food or planning lunch before you've even eaten breakfast? I'm not talking about taking something out of the freezer to thaw for dinner.
2. Do you drive to the other side of town to get that one special something?
3. Do you purchase fourteen donuts because you were supposed to bring home a dozen, and you want to eat two before you get there?
4. Do you sometimes have to go back because you simply couldn't stop at two?
5. Do you hide candy bars in the dresser drawer to be eaten after your significant other goes to sleep or is otherwise occupied?
6. Do you wander the aisles in a grocery store looking for something to satisfy a craving for a little sumpin' sumpin'?

There was a time I could answer yes to all of these questions and more. And if I'm being honest, I still can say yes at times.

That is why sometimes, for me, enough is never enough. That *is* my addiction. Still, I want to stress that this isn't the case for everyone. Each person is different, and some people overeat on occasion but are not addicted to food and cravings. Sometimes it's just overindulging, like at Thanksgiving. When the meal is finished, it is finished. For addicts, once that first "extra" BLT (bite, lick, or taste) goes into the mouth, it's off to the races.

I received mixed messages about food for as long as I can remember. My grandma told me that I had malnutrition when my dad and I first came to live with them as a baby, and she had to fatten me up, which continued right up to the time Dad and I moved. My parents disagreed on how much food should be on our plates. Dad made us clean off our plates, leaving no crumbs, and Mom wanted to limit my food because she thought I was too fat.

From Snack to Binge

As my life moved forward from age ten until age fifty-five, my weight was always going up and down. I had bouts of binging, sometimes lasting weeks or months at a time. I used food to numb my pain after traumatic events. That included when my mom's friend sang the Susan Mae ditty, and I also binged during the aftermath of Ron's infidelity. I was lonely during the long deployments when Ron was away, so I ate. After my best friend Karen lost the fight for her life, I binged while grieving. It was the same after the estrangement with my son and his family. I didn't get heavy overnight, and I haven't fed my addiction by overeating every day.

In between binges, I tried a variety of diets, including counting carbs and calories. Next came Weight Watchers, which I joined three times, the South Beach diet, and grapefruit. I tried Jenny Craig twice, and then TOPS. My weight yo-yoed a lot, with my highest weight reaching 268 pounds.

I was creative and deceptive when I picked up a fork so I could bend my elbow to put food into my mouth. I hid how much I ate from my family. My late-night rendezvous with my creation of triple-decker peanut butter, raisin, and banana sandwiches went down my gullet smoothly, always accompanied by a diet soda.

During my Weight Watcher days, I wrote up a food plan for a week at a time. I planned for a Weight Watchers breakfast "cheesecake" for four days. After the first serving, I liked it so much that I ate the other three days' worth. Because it was written down on my menu plan for that week, I made a second cheesecake. I then reasoned that I could have another serving right then because I only needed three days' worth, and I would put the remainder in the freezer to be pulled out as needed. I'm here to tell you it tasted mighty fine frozen as well.

Binging brought me significant health consequences. My knees hurt, and I had Type 2 diabetes, neuropathy, and high cholesterol. I saw myself headed down a slippery slope with the same health issues as many in my family had.

I had an aunt who weighed over three hundred pounds and went on countless diets. She had bariatric surgery, after which her body developed many food intolerances. At age forty, she needed a wheelchair from complications, partially due to her weight issues after her knee replacement surgery. Her passing was the end result of all of her health issues, beginning with her weight.

My aunt was not the only sufferer, and neither was I. There have been many studies completed on obesity, and thousands more are being conducted as you read this. Unfortunately, here in the United States, you only have to look around to see that we are a nation of people who could certainly benefit from eating healthier. Obesity has become an epidemic. And from what I have read, the trend spans the globe and is now in many countries.

Per Mayo Clinic, "obesity is a complex disease involving excessive body fat. Obesity isn't just a cosmetic concern. It's a medical problem that increases the risk of other diseases and health problems, such as heart disease, diabetes, high blood pressure, and certain cancers."[26]

Finding Answers

Then in 2017, I came across an announcement for one of those free ten-day webinars that popped up in my Facebook feed—hosted by Jon McMahon, who was morbidly obese. He told the story of being at a bonfire on the beach with friends when his shoes caught fire from sitting too close, but he didn't notice the heat on his feet because his neuropathy was so bad, he couldn't feel the pain.

When Jon researched issues related to obesity, food manufacturing, and eating whole food for better nutrition, there wasn't a one-stop shop to find information that had been shared between doctors or with the public. Because of *that* experience at the beach party, he made it his mission to interview people whose work has been related to obesity and to share his findings with the world.

During his webinar, I heard an interview Jon did with Susan Pierce Thompson, PhD, author of *Bright Line Eating, The Science of Living Happy, Thin & Free*.[27] I caught my breath. There were details she disclosed about the human body that held me spellbound. Susan is a tenured adjunct associate professor of brain and cognitive science at the University of Rochester. During the interview, she spoke about willpower and its depletion as we go through the day, making us feel exhausted in today's world. We make so many decisions that we don't have enough willpower left to resist ordering pizza instead of cooking something healthy at the end of the day. It's called decision-making depletion, and I totally understand that facet from my own weight history journey.

Inspired by her words and the science behind her program (and an increase of my blood sugar levels during a recent visit to my doctor), she got my attention. I bought her book and signed up for a boot camp starting on December 1, 2017. That was the day I began my Bright Line Eating journey to address my food addiction. It changed my life in so many ways besides my weight loss. It brought me back to sanity.

At a conference for Bright Line eaters, Susan Pierce Thompson, PhD showed pictures of PET scans showing how sugar can be as addictive as crack cocaine. The scans showed how the brain "lights" up, in the same way, whether from sugar or cocaine. I craved the dopamine hit I got from eating high quantities of sugary foods. Because I spent years feeding my food addiction by eating candy and sweets, foods with sauces, etc., my brain has become hardwired, so to speak, to crave those substances. When I don't eat them, my cravings intensify if I do indulge in a cookie. It's tough for me not to consume the whole bag of cookies because it's hard for me to stop once I start.

As a food addict, it has not been an easy or smooth journey for me to navigate my food program. I rely on a lot of support from the Bright Line Eating (BLE) community. I attend virtual Twelve Step meetings specifically for people who follow the BLE program. I was also given access to a workshop as part of my boot camp showcasing the work of Michael Blackstone.

Left and Right-Side Hemispheres in the Brain

For over thirty years, Michael Blackstone was an interpersonal transformation coach. He used his skills to help his clients transform their performance in the workplace. He noticed, however, that they were miserable in their personal lives, suffering from internal conflicts.

Blackstone read about the discovery made by Nobel Prize winner, Roger Sperry, a psychobiologist, who proved that the brains of humans are of two minds. Sperry found that the human brain has specialized functions on the right and left hemispheres and that the two sides can operate practically independently.[28]

I took a workshop by Michael Blackstone. In it, I discovered that the corpus callosum is a C-shaped nerve fiber bundle that functions like a switchboard operator or liaison, if you will, connecting both the left and right hemispheres in the brain. The corpus callosum was surgically split in the 1940s as a solution to giving patients relief from epileptic seizure activity.

Mr. Blackstone hypothesized the internal conflict his clients were experiencing was due to a disconnect between the two hemispheres not working together. Each hemisphere wanted to run the show independently, therefore causing internal conflict. He created the "Unifying Your Mind" a process of personal reconciliation and reunion. After taking his clients through the process, Blackstone discovered that they all reported their lives dramatically improved in both their professional and personal lives.

It made sense to me how the personal reconciliation and reunion could allow someone to process any, "*do I, don't I?*" (eat that donut) situations they might be struggling to overcome. Not surprisingly, these are usually as a result of a trauma they have gone through sometime during childhood. Communication between each hemisphere ceased to exist, resulting in each side trying to run the show as a way to protect from further hurt.

During the exercise, I closed my eyes as instructed, and I put my hands on my lap, palm side up. The idea was that each hand represented each hemisphere. When they touched, the process of linking hands together signified their agreement to work together.

I was instructed to silently ask what each hemisphere wanted to be called during the meditation. My right creative side declared she was "Madi" and my serious side wanted to be recognized as "Susan." As a third-party participant, I would be involved in the conversation, sort of like an emcee (my higher self). I then asked each side if they were willing to agree to work together and to discuss what outcome they each wanted in any given situation.

Suddenly, I felt my hands touching each other, which startled me. I opened my eyes, and sure enough, my fingers were now interlocked. I knew both sides had indeed agreed to work together instead of each fighting to be in charge!

Even after doing the exercise, I doubted my brain would operate differently. And then, as I was driving home in my car, listening to Pink, suddenly, inside my head, I heard Madi declare, "We should go to Swiss Days in Midway on Saturday. We've never been!"

Susan responded, "Oh no, we shouldn't. There's nothing but sugary treats there; it's not good for our food program!"

"But it will be so much fun," Madi pleaded.

It surprised me at first, but then I realized that the two were working out a compromise as I listened to the rest of the conversation. Madi wanted to have a fun time, and Susan wanted to stay on our food program. They agreed it would be fun to stop and get some iced tea and then take our dog Abby to the park and swing on the swing set instead. We did and had a glorious time.

I promise the story of Bright Line Eating is not intended to be a commercial but an honest description of my personal journey. BLE isn't for everyone, any more than some other ways of eating, but it is working for me.

I still call upon Madi and Susan to solve problem issues. I also use the additional methods Mr. Blackstone has created to craft a peaceful way for solutions. Mr. Blackstone's contact information is listed in the bibliography.

The Food Traps

We are inundated every day with food choices anywhere the eye can see. Some options are blatantly evident, and many of them are subliminal. Food cues are everywhere, competing for our attention, but more importantly, for our wallets' folded green things.

I live in a large metropolitan area with over 1.24 million people. I can't drive down a street without seeing a fast food or a sit-down restaurant holding space in a parking lot, the signage dotting the landscape with multitudes of colors vying for my attention.

Food is such a part of our culture. Family gatherings, holiday celebrations, weddings, funerals, and even board meetings all have opportunities to eat. Unlike other substances and addictive behaviors like shopping or gambling that people use to numb pain from emotions, we need food to *survive*. That makes it tough: we can't resolve the addiction because if there is no food, there is no life.

In social situations, if someone is an alcoholic and friends or family are aware of the addiction, most people won't offer them a beer. However, if you are trying to watch what you eat, how often do you hear, "Oh, just one piece won't hurt you!"?

Inundated with Advertising

During the 2022 Super Bowl, out of the twenty commercials I reviewed, there were ads for food or drink eighty-eight times, sometimes as many as five or six examples in each commercial. Some things were positioned on a counter or in the background during the main advertisement within the commercial. Each of these sends out subliminal messages encouraging us to purchase the product the next time we shop.

I became curious about the marketing strategy companies that sell these strategies to food manufacturers to entice the consumer to buy their products. My first Google search garnered an entire page with multiple listings for large companies in business to help companies in the food industry increase their bottom line. Michael Moss's book, *Salt Sugar Fat. How Food Giants Hooked Us.*[29]

Food Dive is a leading industry publication operated by Industry Dive. An article by Jessi Devenyns in *Food Dive* states, "Nostalgia is a growing trend as consumers lean on brands that pull on their heartstrings during the pandemic. This appeal has, in recent years, been especially strong in the cereal category as brands look to appeal to indulgent childhood favorites to reinvigorate sales."

Final Thoughts on How to Navigate Through Food Issues

Write your answers on the available note page at the end of this chapter.

- Is there a particular time of day or situation that may be a trigger for you to eat something to soothe an emotion?
- Do you have a particular food you are drawn to when you *do* get triggered?
- How important is it that food will be served at a social gathering?
- What emotions come up for you after any indulgent behavior?
- Are there health concerns or conditions affecting your life?
- How might a change in your eating habits serve your physical or mental health or both?

If you find yourself craving something that you know you do not need:

1. Center yourself and breathe. Find something else to distract yourself and wait twenty minutes; the craving will usually disappear.
2. Find a buddy you can reach out to or do an activity together.
3. In a social situation when a buffet is offered, spend time getting to know someone new instead of perusing the food table.

Most importantly, don't beat yourself up if you eat something you weren't planning on eating. Whatever food program you choose to follow, please be gentle with yourself. It can be challenging, but you can do it. Positive self-talk is one of the most important things you can do for yourself.

CHAPTER SEVENTEEN

Wielding a Wicked Rag

You have to decide whether you're going to let your
past destroy you or whether you're going to let it build
you into the strongest person you've ever met.
—Sonya Parker

How farfetched was the idea for me to forgive all of the people who had wronged me? How much of a reach did I make? Did it take courage? The thought of doing any of those things certainly seemed ludacris. But forgiving didn't happen quickly, that's for sure. To forgive someone doesn't mean you are condoning what happened because it suddenly becomes okay. It's not, however, what happened for me when I was finally able to forgive those who hurt me, which gave me a new sense of well-being. Peace and serenity took up residency in my heart.

Dad and Mom had only been married a couple of months when it was apparent to me she had a routine she expected me to follow to the letter. At seven years old, I was still trying to make the adjustment of having a mom that always barked orders and snide remarks at me.

Mom had a personality the likes of Jekyll and Hyde. It was never more apparent than on Saturdays, "chore" day. It was in early spring 1958, while I was getting dressed, I wondered what kind of mood she would be in. If she were in a good mood, the list of chores would be short. It was her bad mood days I dreaded. It always ended the same way. I got yelled at because I didn't clean well enough and was always declared a spoiled snot. Randy, on the other hand, never did chores. Mom always picked up his dirty clothes and made his bed for him.

One such Saturday before I had to set my eyes on her, I slowly wandered into the kitchen, looking to soothe my parched throat. I chugged down a glass of cherry Kool-Aid, poured myself a bowl of Frosted Flakes, and sat alone, enjoying the calm before the possible storm.

I didn't have to wait too long. Mom slid through the doorway dressed for the day. She was dressed in a blue and white house dress over her swimsuit for lying on the chaise lounge to work on her tan. Trailing behind was her dog Snoopy, a fuzzy-haired Pomeranian. Shooting daggers with her eyes and speaking in an abrasive tone, she asked, "Are you going to just sit there drinking that 'rotgut' and stuffing your face all day?"

Inside, I shrunk. Hearing that tone in her voice, I knew what was in store for me *that* day.

The biggest difference between myself and Cinder from *Cinderella* was that I didn't have the cheerful birds and mice to help and keep me company. *I* didn't get to sing and dance around while I worked.

In fact, when I did sing, my mom made fun of me. "Quit singing!" she'd gripe. "You can't carry a tune in a bucket." Adding insult to injury, she'd say, "It hurts my ears, so knock it off."

Armed with my rag and a boatload of determination, I headed to the bathroom in our small two-bedroom red brick house to start my cleaning.

The standard operating procedure was that after I finished "cleaning," my work would be inspected. No matter how much time I took or how well I cleaned, Mom always told me to do it again because it was never good enough. But that morning, I told myself I'd show her!

I held the rag by the corner, swooshing it around in the toilet bowl, making sure that the noise was loud enough so Mom could hear me "clean."

I absentmindedly started singing, to which she promptly yelled from the other room: "Get busy in there and quit singing!"

I straightened up, pushing my shoulders back, muttering under my breath, "I *can to sing. I don't care what she says. I'm so tired of her picking on me.*"

When I finished, I called out, "I'm done!"

Acting like the inspector general in the army, she marched into the room. Her face was already displaying a sneer, despite what seemed like what had been an hour on hands and knees on the floor, scrubbing the toilet, sink, and tub.

After seeing the look on her face, I held my breath, bracing myself for what I knew was coming next:

"Do it again!" she ordered.

I was boiling inside as she left. *I'm really going to show her now,* I thought. I took the rag and plunged it into the toilet bowl again, generating more noise than before. I scrubbed harder than ever, moving my rag in circles so fast it was as if I were churning cream to make butter.

I'll show her a thing or two! I repeated silently to myself.

After the second inspection was completed, she anticipated the words that were coming even before she uttered them. "See, if you had done it right in the first place, you wouldn't have to clean it twice. Now get out of here and go play."

Through clenched teeth, I seethed, "See how much you know! That *was* my first time scrubbing it!" I bravely continued, "I knew you would make me do it over, as always, so I only cleaned it once."

"Oh, really now? How clever you think you are," Mom snarled. "There *will* be no playing today. Go to your room; you're grounded!"

"That's not fair!" Lowering my head, I added, "I think you love Snoopy more than me."

"Yes," she retorted. "As a matter of fact, I do."

My face fell. I knew it was true, but it hurt that she would admit she loved the dog more than me–and say it out loud. Then my mom deliberately poured more salt on my already wounded heart.

"Snoopy doesn't give me all the guff you do, and *she's* quiet!"

Hot, wet tears streamed down my face. I sniffled, then blurted out, "You're going to be in big, big trouble when I tell my dad what you said."

Mom looked at me with stone-cold blue eyes. "Oh . . . I doubt that."

Great. Not only am I expected to stay in my room, but there will be no IronPort soda.

Normally I would reward myself after enduring the tirade from my wicked stepmom. It was usually late morning by the time I finished my chores. I would walk to the local corner grocery store, and it felt like

I was on parole from being on house arrest. Breathing the fresh air always renewed my soul.

I anticipated the refreshing IronPort soda cascading down my throat when I swallowed. It was like a cold waterfall exploding in my mouth from the bubbles of the carbonated water.

Running to my room, I threw myself on my bed. Crying crocodile tears of deep sadness, I wept and wondered what the dog had that I didn't. Was it because Snoopy wiggled around when someone talked to her? Or because she showed her love for Mom all the time? I could wiggle around! I hadn't had a mom in my life, and I desperately *wanted* to have her look at me the same way she looked at Snoopy. Why was I so unlovable? I didn't understand.

Everything will be better when Dad finds out, I thought. *We will go back to Grandma's house where we belong.* Only I wasn't able to tell Dad until the next day because my parents went bowling after dinner. Still, when I was able to talk to him, Dad had a distracted look on his face as he promised he would talk to Mom when he had a minute. That really demonstrated how low on the totem pole I was in his life. *When he has a minute usually never comes,* I thought.

Two weeks later, absolutely nothing had changed. It didn't get any better. It was clear there would be no going back to Grandma's house, as much as I wanted to.

I don't think he even bothered to talk to Mom. More time passed, and the only option I had was to suck it up. I learned to depend on myself and spent as much time as I could in my backyard alone. Randy was usually off with his friends.

I thought about how things were so good at my grandma's house. When we lived with her, we went to church every week. I missed the church connection I had with my friends. I asked Dad if we could start going to church in hopes of finding a connection with the other girls my age like I had once known while living at Grandma's. His response? "We'll see." Nothing changed on that front either.

Once I reached my teenage years, I avoided my mom as much as possible and didn't have much to do with her the rest of the time I lived at home. When I got my Volkswagen at age seventeen, I spent as much time as I could anywhere else but home. I couldn't wait to leave and be rid of her and her mean words and moved out and away as soon as possible.

At age nineteen, I learned I was pregnant with my daughter. Two months later, Mom was diagnosed with a Stage 4 brain tumor. Within two days, she was on the surgical table. The prognosis she was given after surgery was about six months. Although it turned out she did survive for almost ten more years, the radiation and chemotherapy left her with physical and cognitive limitations.

During those ten years, we came home to Utah for visits as often as possible. I loved coming "home" and introducing my children to my favorite places. I witnessed how the relationship between my daughter and Mom blossomed. On the last visit before she passed, they baked cookies together. I saw the tenderness in Mom's eyes when she looked at my daughter. I was happy for both of them.

Having worked with patients with disabilities over the years, I've watched patients who had to endure being talked down to or totally ignored. I was able to look at Mom through more compassionate eyes after witnessing my dad's cruelty and the way he bullied her since she became ill. It was hard for me to watch. Showing his narcissism, Dad made jokes in front of people about the mistakes she made, like when she unplugged the freezer because the temperature read thirty degrees. For the first time in my life, I felt protective of her.

Christmas Wallet

On one such visit at Mom's request, I took her to a department store so she could purchase a wallet for Dad for Christmas. It took her over thirty minutes to select just the right one. She proudly stood at the counter filling out her check, but the task proved to be more of a challenge than she could handle. Mom's limited use of her right hand (the dominant one) had significantly decreased due to the atrophy resulting from the brain surgery six years prior.

After a few minutes, the clerk shifted her weight impatiently from one foot to the other, displaying her annoyance at it taking so long. With an exasperated tone in her voice, the clerk said, "Don't you have a credit card? You're holding up the line 'cuz you're so slow!"

Mom now wore a mortified expression on her face. "I'm so sorry," was all she could manage, while dropping her head down.

As I watched her, my heart ached as I witnessed the inhumane treatment this clerk was dishing out to her. Gently lifting Mom's face, I looked her in the eye and quietly suggested, "Why don't you let me finish filling this out, then you can sign it?"

She nodded as tears welled up in her eyes. As soon as she finished signing the check, she stepped away from the counter, and showing her embarrassment, she headed toward the door. I let her go . . . so I could have a word with the rude young lady. Looking at her name tag, I informed Kathy I would be calling the manager when I got home. I didn't want to delay getting Mom out of there.

As we slowly walked to the car, Mom said, "I feel so stupid to have taken so much time." She paused and added, "I wanted to buy you lunch. That's the least I could do for you to bring me to the store, but your dad doesn't ever let me have any cash. He tells me I don't need any because I get too confused and all I had with me is a check."

At that moment, sympathy overwhelmed me. I had a flashback of all the times I had to sit and wait to get my allowance from Dad, remembering how controlling he was when it came to shelling out any of the money he owed me that was rightfully earned. Apparently, he did the same thing to his wife as well.

That night, when Dad got home from work, I confronted him. "How dare you not give Mom any money, knowing I was taking her shopping today!" I was fuming inside.

True to form, Dad made excuses whenever he got called out on something. He stammered, "I didn't know you were going out today."

Feeling appalled, I fired back, "Yes, you did! You knew I was going to take her shopping today. I told you last night." Glaring at him, I added, "She just wanted to get *your* Christmas present." *Not that you deserve one!*

I turned on my heel, walking away, hoping Dad would finally realize how thoroughly disgusted I was with him.

The next evening, Mom and I watched television together. My dad had gone to a meeting for church. *Eight Is Enough* was playing, one of her favorite television programs. As soon as it was over, I knew it was getting close to her bedtime of nine o'clock, so I suggested that she start getting ready for bed. It usually took her a while due to the decline in her strength and stamina.

When I checked on her about thirty minutes later, I noticed she was still sitting on the toilet, tears streaming down her face.

"What's wrong?" I asked as I touched her knee.

She looked at me and simply said, "He's going to kill me."

"What are you talking about?" I asked.

"I dropped my toothbrush down the furnace vent," she said, her eyes wide and scared, "and he's just going to kill me." She was now crying uncontrollably.

My heart broke for her. As I looked over at the sink, I noticed a toothbrush sitting in the holder and pointed it out to her.

"Oh no," she replied, "that's my morning toothbrush." Snot streaming from her nose, she just repeated over and over while shaking her head, "He's just going to kill me, he's just going to kill me."

I had another intense wave of compassion rise over me toward this woman. She had not been very kind to me all those years, but as my mother, as a human, and as my father's loyal companion, she deserved respect. As I helped her wipe her nose, I realized how much my dad's abuse had diminished this once proud, capable person to a broken woman.

I couldn't help but see myself in the expression in her eyes red from crying. I could now see what the years of his narcissism and obvious mistreatment had done to her–I was able to get away from what I thought was a cesspool of painful existence caused by both. In that moment, I realized Mom had been a victim of Dad's abuse as well. I no longer saw her as my wicked stepmom. I only saw a woman who deserved compassion and love.

I knew I needed to let go of any of the remaining bitterness and anger I still was harboring toward her. I needed to love her as *I* had so desperately wanted to be loved. After Mom died, I came to understand in her own way, she did love me. She had spent so many hours decorating my bedroom, and sewing school clothes for me, even though I detested her choices of styles in both areas. I hadn't given her any credit for the things she had done for me. It no longer mattered if, in the past, she was unable to express her love for me with words.

I thought about the time when I was in high school as a passenger in my friend's car. I received a minor injury in a terrible car accident when one of my friends lost his life. Mom really showed up for me with compassion. She ran interference for me from all the phone calls with people's nosey questions wanting to know all the gory details about what had happened. Memory after memory came forward because I had healed enough of the bad ones to have room for the good memories.

The Relationship with Mom Had Three Phases, Beginning, Middle, and An End

In previous chapters, I talked about my awareness and the necessity to take responsibility for my own actions. After making corrections in my behavior, another layer of awareness would quite often show up. Living through all of the tortuous years I endured at the hands of my stepmom, I viewed myself as a victim. I wore a red cloak of victimhood proudly. I now see clearly my healing journey began in earnest while sitting in the rooms in my Al-Anon meetings.

Phase one of the relationship with my mom began when my dad married her. I recounted my side of the story over and over to anyone who would listen. I was looking for sympathy and advice. I kept busy recruiting people to join Team Sue, and eventually Team Madison, to stand with me. Deep inside, I didn't believe I was smart enough to figure things out on my own. Yet a part of me didn't want a solution; I just wanted the attention and understanding I hadn't receive as a child. The emotional pain from my past remained in the background while driving my bus through life. The transition from the first phase to the second didn't happen overnight.

At the beginning of the second phase with Mom, I had developed some life skills as an adult, wherein I began to take ownership of my piece of the relationship with her. I started to understand how I wore my attitude and bitterness on my sleeve. I realized it couldn't have been very pleasant to be around my negative energy either. I also recognized how my learned behaviors had shaped my beliefs about what had happened to me and why. I slowly began to let a sliver of anguish go. I could see the need for compassion for other people, especially since Mom had physical and cognitive impairments.

Entering the third phase of our relationship took place during the last years of my mom's life. I had witnessed her increasing physical and emotional decline. I began to see how my narcissistic dad treated her with the same disrespect and cruelty he had done to me and others. I saw a frail woman who deserved to be treated better and deserved my compassion and forgiveness. It wasn't about condoning what had happened to me and forget about it. I will always have unpleasant memories of that part of my life, but I don't feel the emotional impact on me when I think about them like they once had. And the positive ones kept coming back.

At about that time, I also experienced a resurgence of interest in my spiritual development. Allowing God to work in my life was a game-changer for me. Reciting the ho'oponopono prayer became a powerful practice on my healing journey with this mom, too, and with the mom inside of me who had made mistakes as well.

Things to Consider

- Have you taken the stance of victimhood as your identity?
- Do you feel justified in playing the part of the victim?
- Are you stuck in phase one, always thinking about it?
- It's essential to consider the entire story or history in phases and determine if you are stuck in phase one or phase two so you can know what it might take for you to move forward.

- Forgiveness can lessen emotional baggage because you are no longer spending time dwelling on the issue.
- Forgiveness can give back your power.

CHAPTER EIGHTEEN

Anger to Peace, One Layer at a Time

"If you're going to clean a house, you're going have to see the dirt first."
—Louise Hay

When I received the email bombshell from my son declaring I was a narcissist, I knew it was time for me to "clean house." My dirt came to the surface, knocking at my door, grabbing my attention, and compelling me to discover all the learned behaviors along my journey. It prompted me to investigate and determine if I *was* a narcissist. I shared the results with complete candor and vulnerability, despite how difficult the road had been. After I realized it was imperative to look at my own contributions to my negative attitude, I became more conscientious about the words that came out of my mouth. It's now an ongoing practice.

What Is Energetic Vibration? And Why Is It So Important to Understand?

Healing your emotional, mental, physical, and spiritual life takes time. It doesn't happen overnight. Peeling back each layer of the emotional traumas *you* have or may still be feeling one at a time will help you release the old chains you may have been bound by–beliefs about yourself or labels from others.

What you may discover, as I have, is that this raises your energetic vibration when you let go of any animosity you may be holding on to. And in doing so, you will gain increased clarity and tranquility, allowing you to move forward with your life more easily. Let's dive into what exactly "energetic vibration" is and what techniques you can use to make things so much lighter and more beautiful for you.

"Everything in life is vibration," Albert Einstein.

Everything in the universe is made up of molecules vibrating at different speeds. This includes trees, bodies, rocks, animals, thoughts, and emotions. Human vibrations are composed of everything from physical matter to the way you communicate the thoughts you think. In simple terms, some molecules vibrate faster and some vibrate slower; there are higher vibrations and lower vibrations.

Your body is composed of energy-producing particles, each of which is in constant motion. So, like everything and everyone else in the universe, you are vibrating and creating energy all of the time.

Every time you recognize and process your layers of trauma, you will increase this energetic vibration. You will find the cobwebs in your mind will be swept away, so you too will have more clarity due to the absence of prior webs that caught you and brought you down.

What's commonly discovered is that our old skin doesn't fit anymore. The patterns, behaviors, and old labels that have now been stripped away no longer apply to our lives.

You may find the new skin isn't entirely comfortable yet. And sometimes, when trauma or hurt runs deep, you might have to process those things more than once. Most of my friends, my clients, and myself have learned that we have certain hurts that will show up again. It can make us say, "Wait, what? I've already dealt with this! What the @%$*?"

Don't let that keep you from making your way through each layer. They each play an important role.

A year and a half after my divorce from Ron, I became very bitter and angry all over again when I thought about infidelity. After going to my Twelve Step meetings for about a year, I discovered there were more layers of anger I needed to process. I was relieved to learn that this was, in fact, normal. Each time that negative emotion came up, the intensity was less *because* I had done a lot of healing in my emotional, physical, mental, and spiritual life. Through those groups and reiki, I was able to finally release the toxic energy from my divorce and the aftermath I had been packing around like heavy boulders in a backpack.

Many Layers Later . . .

My eyes are now completely wide open . . . well, okay, *most* of the time. Not long ago, I was in my quiet space to meditate and do my morning writing. I was looking forward to catching up with a close friend and meeting her granddaughter for lunch.

Before I headed out, I needed to make several phone calls. One of those calls was to cancel the lawn service we had. My husband and I were unhappy with the product they used on our lawn because it had burned the grass, making it uncomfortable on the bottoms of our bare feet.

When a woman answered the phone, I said in a pleasant voice, "I think your company's product has burned our grass. Last fall, our lawn looked great, and now it's almost dead. I want to cancel our contract, please."

She replied, but with a condescending tone, "We have thousands of customers who are satisfied with our service and never complain about our products." Raising her voice, she added, "You must not be watering correctly!"

That made me sit back in my chair, shocked. I felt judged and verbally belittled as if it were my dad speaking to me. I found myself raising my voice to match hers in my response: "I *know,* we are having a drought, so everyone is watering less. However, I think I know how to water my grass just fine!"

She challenged my statement. "Lady, you *can't* be watering correctly, or the grass would be in great condition."

By now, I was beside myself. I had knots in my stomach because I was so pissed. "I don't want you to make any more applications," I demanded, "because your company's product *is* killing the lawn, and you need to cancel our contract as of today."

She eventually agreed to cancel our service only after I threatened to file a complaint with the Better Business Bureau. Even though I was successful, I was rattled, nonetheless. Our contract was cancelled, and we went with a different service.

As I got ready to leave the house for my lunch date, I put the phone call out of my mind because I was focusing on what I wanted to create for the rest of my day. I had other plans besides my lunch date.

I would be getting my wedding ring fixed after we had lunch and was glad because then I wouldn't have to worry about losing the stone that had recently become loose. I had been nervous, almost paranoid, about it for several days now and was relieved to have time to fix it. I met my friend and her granddaughter. We had a lovely time catching up over soup and sandwiches. We parted ways with hugs and smiles, promising to get together soon. My vibration was high again.

After leaving the restaurant, I went to the jeweler where we had purchased my wedding ring. I recently needed to resize the ring and had a spring put inside the band. Unfortunately, the stone had come loose around the same time, so I wanted them to tighten it so the stone wouldn't fall out.

"I need to have the stone tightened, please." I slid the ring through the opening in the window so he could examine it. After inspecting it, he informed me they could fix it, but there would be a fee.

I was dumbfounded. "I don't understand. Less than a month ago, I brought my ring in to be resized. Why would it be loose now unless the prongs weren't tightened enough when you worked on it?"

He said, "Lady, I don't know what you have done to cause that."

"I didn't do anything. Why would you charge me to fix it? Don't you guarantee your work?"

Shoving my ring back under the glass toward me, he retorted, "Lady, I can't help you with *that* attitude." He then turned on his heel, dismissing me, and walked away.

Raising my voice, I called after him, "I will be giving your store a Google review, and it will not be a good one!"

I walked away feeling unheard and dismissed for the second time that day, just like I had felt many times after having a conversation with Dad. Fuming inside while walking to my car, the knots from that morning reappeared with a vengeance. I was determined that I would write a review of the store and the poor customer service as soon as I returned home. When I got home, I did write a poor review. I took my ring to a different jeweler who repaired it without cost. In the future, I will buy any jewelry from Mike's Custom Made Jewelry in Murray, Utah.

I had been on the road for about ten minutes, still fuming while driving to my next destination. I was ready to rip out someone's throat. It dawned on me at that moment, however, that I had had two altercations in less than four hours. Shaking my head, I had a moment of realization. That's when I admitted to myself what was really going on: *It isn't the people I've had altercations with, but it's me who has contributed to the negative outcome.*

In further reflection, I remembered something that was likely the root of my issue: that morning during my writing time, I had been working on a chapter of this book, covering my dad's narcissism and how he had discounted and belittled me, never letting me feel heard. When I made that phone call and again when I went to the jeweler, I was still carrying that negative energy with me without realizing it!

I continued to give thought to my attitude throughout both incidents. Because of all the deep, inner work I had previously done on myself, I was able to take a step back. Then I got curious as to why the intensity of my anger had spilled out.

I parked my car, did a round of EFT tapping, and applied Balance®, a blend of essential oils on the bottoms of my feet for grounding. Feeling much lighter and calmer, I was able to get on with my day.

By recognizing the need to simply feel what I'm feeling, giving myself permission to sit with it, and using the tools I have shared with you, I have learned to honor myself for doing enough work, so those feelings don't stay with me very long. I can feel the stress and tension in my body dissipate after enjoying meditation and doing some breath work, or using one of the other tools I have written about.

In years past, when I was triggered like this, I would have been an emotional wreck for weeks, if not months, and perhaps even years prior to walking my healing path. That day, it took me only a matter of minutes.

I am very grateful for the mentors and teachers who have shared their knowledge with me as I now share with you.

Through the years, I have come to believe that everything is energy, and the words we say and think have a huge impact on our lives.

Everything has an energetic vibration attached to it. I see how it applies in relationships, reiki, EFT tapping, and many other healing modalities, even ones I haven't discussed here in this book.

I continue to stay curious about behaviors and the reasons behind them. I love to seek out new modalities so I can be more and more effective personally and with my clients. In that way, I am always open to learning new things.

Words We Say and Think Affect Everything

I found a fascinating study on energy patterns and the frequency of vibrations from speaking different words. They have found that thoughts can affect the molecular structure of water, as discussed in the book, *The Hidden Messages in Water* by Masaru Emoto.[30] While some have called him a pseudo-scientist, others have been replicating his studies and discovering even more fascinating truths, particularly in Germany.

Emoto documented his findings. He collected water from many different sources, including spring water, groundwater, and upper river streams, and put them in vials. Emoto even took samples at Angel Valley in Sedona, Arizona, known for its healing water. After exposing the vials to positive and negative words, he froze the water.

Emoto looked at the crystals that were formed under a microscope and discovered pristine shapes with the crystals that were showered with positive words. He discovered those that were given negative or harsh labels, the crystals had jagged edges or didn't form at all.

While I was working at an adult day care center where many of our clients had cognitive disabilities, I ran a science club with simple but profound activities for the clients to help them with their reasoning skills.

Inspired by Emoto's experiments with white rice in jars, we duplicated the experiment using the same methods of speaking positively to one and negatively to another as he did with water. After three months, in the positive word container of cooked white rice, we found the jars had hardly changed color, but the rice in which the negative, harsh words were given had become dark and moldy.

Our limiting beliefs are developed much in the same way, by the words we tell ourselves or what others tell us. Positive and negative words, as we've already talked about in chapter ten, do profoundly affect us.

Lindsey Horton from the Business Relationship Management Institute posted that, "Scientific studies actually show that positive and negative words not only affect us on a *deep psychological level*, but they have a significant impact on the outcome of our lives."

Methods You Can Use to Increase Your Energy Vibrations

Words and thoughts are not the only way to increase your vibration, according to Insight Timer, meditative sleep music with 528Hz solfeggio frequency and 1.5 Hz delta waves (binaural beats). It's designed to help you drift off into a deep sleep, waking up regenerated and rejuvenated.

There are many resources available to find these types of music. Some of them are free and some you need to pay for. See the bibliography for some suggestions.

Music and tones have been used for centuries.

- Ancient Egyptians used a method called "toning." They manipulated the vowel sound using breath and voice to render therapeutic sounds.[31]

- The didgeridoo is an Aboriginal instrument that traditionally is important in Aboriginal ceremonies, where the voice of the didgeridoo was part of storytelling and teaching. It's been found that this extraordinary storytelling instrument can also heal and has been added to many therapeutic songs for its healing vibration alone.[32]

- Tibetan meditation bowls and singing bowls are great tools. Each bowl has its own tone and, when played, emits different sound frequencies that can affect different areas of the body to provide healing.[33]

Here's the moral of this whole story: when we speak harshly to ourselves, those words have a lower vibration. And when we are at a lower vibration, it leaves us wide open for more challenges in our lives. Our outlook on life is like the glass half empty. Negativity always breeds negativity or lower vibrations, but there are multiple ways to bring your energy back into positivity.

As I put into practice the tools I have written about in this book, my energy vibration has gotten higher. I have continually increased my vibration because I choose to do the work, giving me tremendous clarity. There is less clutter in my brain to bog my thoughts down. That doesn't mean I am better than you, it simply means I have more clarity in my life and brain. That allows me to focus on what *is* important to me. I can sit in stillness in meditation and prayer after awakening each morning with cheerful gratitude for my family, health, mental stamina, and spiritual life. I take the time to listen for answers because I have the clarity to do so.

The awareness that you have been triggered by something unrelated to the circumstance or situation helps you work through any additional layers needing to be processed. It gives you the confidence and the wherewithal to realize what issue from your past the frustrations or anger is actually about.

Now that you've gained knowledge and many tools on our journey together, you can begin to recognize how the influences were placed in your petri dish. It may have been during your childhood or as an adult or maybe both. You can give yourself permission to let go of the learned behaviors you may have created as a defense mechanism, raise your vibrations, and create in your inner world and your outer world more love, positivity, and joy.

It really is all about choice—and sometimes just choosing differently.

Do I use all of my tools all of the time? Heavens, no, but I do use them when I need to. Now that you have the same arsenal available, it is my hope you won't have to crash on the rocks of despair that I sank my boat on. You can have a peaceful life in your own lagoon.

And please know, you don't have to do this alone. If you'd like assistance on your journey, with a partner who can walk beside you in learning about yourself and using these healing tools, I am here.

I'd like to invite you to make the same choice I made, as in buckle down and get the work done! It's worth it. Through the process, you'll get closer to successfully building a life full of opportunities. You'll be able to enhance your life and your relationship with yourself. You will also be able to have a greater, more positive impact on loved ones in your life, and begin living more tangibly in your ikigai–your passion and reason for breathing. Isn't it time to create instead of reacting? It's time to claim your place on the planet, once and for all!

Check out my website for information about working with me, and to access my blog, for more information go to : www.madisonfrederick.com.

Bibliography

Chapter Two
[1] What is EMDR?
    https://www.emdr.com/what-is-emdr/.

Chapter Three
[2] https://www.rainn.org.
    RAINN 1-800-656-4673; available 24/7.

Chapter Four: Overcoming Labels
[3] Clear, James. *Atomic Habits: An Easy & Proven Way to Build Good Habits & Break Bad Ones.* (Penguin Random House, 2018.
[4] What is ikigai?
    https://www.betterup.com/blog/what-is-ikigai.

Chapter Seven: Gaslighting
[5] Stern, Dr. Robin. *The Gaslight Effect: How to Spot and Survive the Hidden Manipulation Others Use to Control Your Life.* Harmony Books, 2007.
    https://robinstern.com/
[6] https://www.aetv.com/real-crime/warren-jeffs-now.

Chapter Eight: Codependency
[7] Beattie, Melody. *Codependent No More: How to Stop Controlling Others and Start Caring For Yourself.* Hazelton Publishing, 1986.
[8] https://dramyjohnson.com/habits/relationships-codependency/.
    Johnson, Amy PhD. *The Little Book Of Big Change.* New Harbinger Publications, Inc., 2016.

Chapter Nine: Twelve Step Segway To Self-Awareness

Al-Anon Family Group Headquarters. "One Day at a Time in Al-Anon." January 1, 1987.

https://al-anon.org 2021-Membership.pdf, 8. Currently, there are over 24,000 Al-Anon groups and nearly 1,500 Alateen groups meeting in 118 countries.

[9] Gamblers Anonymous: https://www.gamblersanonymous.org/ga.

[10] Overeaters Anonymous: https://oa.org/.

[11] Cocaine Anonymous: https://ca.org./

[12] Adult Children of Alcoholics: https://adultchildren.org/.

[13] Debtors Anonymous: https://debtorsanonymous.org/.

[14] Narcotics Anonymous: https://na.org/.

[15] Codependent anonymous https://coda.org. (co-dependents anonymous?

[16] What is EFT tapping? Emotion Freedom Technique.

https://www.everydayhealth.com/wellness/eft-tapping/guide/#:~:-text=What%20does%20EFT%20tapping%20do,cravings%2C%20and%20help%20resolve%20fears.

Chapter Ten: Importance of Play

[17] Bradshaw, John PhD. *Homecoming: Reclaiming and Championing Your Inner Child*, Bantam Books. August, 1990.

[18] What Is Forest Bathing? (shinrin-yoku)

https://pubmed.ncbi.nlm.nih.gov/19568835/#:~:text=The%20term%20Shinrin%2Dyoku%20was,the%20atmosphere%20of%20the%20forest.

[19] https://news.harvard.edu/gazette/story/2017/04/over-nearly-80-years-harvard-study-has-been-showing-how-to-live-a-healthy-and-happy-life/.

Robert Waldinger, director of the study, a psychiatrist at Massachusetts General Hospital, and a professor of psychiatry at Harvard Medical School. Harvard study, almost eighty years old, has proved that embracing community helps us live longer and be happier.

Chapter Eleven: Let Go And Let God

[20] Kubler-Ross, Elizabeth. *On Death And Dying.* Scribner, 1969. Elisabeth Kübler-Ross teachings https://grief.com/the-five-stages-of-grief/.

[21] What Is Reiki? https://www.reiki.org/faqs/what-reiki.

Chapter Twelve: Embrace Your Inner Child

[22] https://www.newworldencyclopedia.org/entry/Automatic_writing.

Chapter Fourteen: Forgiving Narcissism . . . and Other Human Frailties

[23] The ho'oponopono prayer. https://healingbrave.com/blogs/all/hooponopono-prayer-for -forgiveness

Chapter Fifteen: No Contact Clause

[24] Brooks, David. "What's Ripping American Families Apart?" *New York Times,* July 29, 2021. https://www.nytimes.com/2021/07/29/opinion/estranged-ameri-can-families.html.

[25] *Ibid.*

Chapter Sixteen: Forgiveness Enough Is Never Enough

[26] https://www.mayoclinic.org/diseases-conditions/obesity/symptoms -causes/syc-20375742

[27] *Bright Line Eating, The Science of Living Happy, Thin & Free.* Hay House Inc., March 21, 2017. https://www.fooddive.com/news/with-80s-cereal-formulations-gen-eral-mills-goes-back-to-the-future/585633/.

[28] Michael Blackstone, Mentor International Inc. Phoenix, Arizona. https://www.linkedin.com/in/michaelblackstone/.

[29] *Bright Line Eating, The Science of Living Happy, Thin & Free.* Hay House Inc., March 21, 2017.

https://www.fooddive.com/news/with-80s-cereal-formulations-general-mills-goes-back-to-the-future/585633/.

Chapter Eighteen: Anger to Peace One Layer At A Time

[30] Emoto, Masaru. *Water Crystal Healing: Music and Images to Restore Your Well-Being*. Atria Books, October 17, 2006.

[31] Sound healing
Sai Priankaa B. December 21, 2018.
https://www.soulveda.com/wellbeing/sound-healing-in-ancient-egypt/.

[32] Aboriginal instrument didgeridoo
http://www.walkaboutpark.com.au/aboriginal-culture/didgeridoo.

[33] Benefits of singing bowls
Vilhena, Mariana Da. *Meditation Bowls: Singing Bowls for Beginners and Chakras Healing*. Healmonic Publishing, 2022.

Appendix

Why Essential Oils

When purchasing essential oils, it is important to choose pure oils. I use Doterra CPTG ® (certified pure therapeutic grade) because of its purity, and there are no added constituents like fillers or solvents.

The sense of smell is closely tied to the centers of the brain that deal with emotions; inhaling the aroma of essential oils is one of the most powerful ways to affect emotions. There are several methods to use the oils. The first is aromatically, simply smelling directly from the bottle or putting a few drops in a diffuser. You can also apply them topically. They can be pretty potent, so using a carrier oil such as fractionated coconut oil can increase absorption and efficacy. Drop directly under the tongue or in a gel cap to take the oils internally. Read the label for warnings of non-internal use.

While writing this book, there were more layers of emotions stirred up. I needed to process the residuals of emotions left behind from the many traumas I experienced. The list of essential oils below is just a few I used while processing my memories of the traumas I endured many years before.

- I used Serenity® to help me accept the situation of my estrangement with my son.
- Lavender assisted me in communicating my thoughts on paper. In addition, lavender has a calming effect.
- The many citrus oils, lime, lemon, wild orange, and grapefruit helped uplift my mood, ease my anxiety, and reduce my frustration levels.
- Diffusing clove was helpful when digging back into my memories,

and I was writing about my boundaries or lack of.

- Copaiba helps bring clarity and forgiveness.
- Diffusing frankincense while writing the second letter to my birth mom helped me process the shame I felt because of the ulterior motive I had when I wrote the first letter.
- Vetiver can help with discovering your life purpose and embracing life to the fullest.

To learn more about essential oils, go to my website: www.madisonfrederick.com.

Resources

Chapter Two: He, Himself, and Him
https://www.youtube.com/watch?v=J4yraZiJ9D8.
Ramani S. Durvasula, PhD
Statistics on narcissism

https://www.therecoveryvillage.com/mental-health/narcissistic-personality
-disorder/npd-statistics

Chapter Three: The Betrayal of Trust
https://www.nsvrc.org
National Sexual Violence Resource Center 1-877-739-3895.

https://centerforfamilyjustice.org
Domestic Abuse Hotline 203-384-9559.
Sexual Assault Hotline 203-333-2233.

Chapter Nine: Twelve Steps of Alcoholics Anonymous
https://www.aa.org/
Other organizations utilizing the Twelve Steps of Alcoholics Anonymous:
- Gamblers Anonymous: https://www.gamblersanonymous.org/ga.
- Overeaters Anonymous: https://oa.org/.
- Cocaine Anonymous: https://ca.org/.
- Adult Children of Alcoholics: https://adultchildren.org/.
- Debtors Anonymous: https://debtorsanonymous.org/.
- Narcotics Anonymous: https://na.org/.
- Codependent anonymous https://coda.org. (co-dependents anonymous?.

https://www.samhsa.gov (the substance abuse and mental health services administration).

Chapter Ten: There Is More to Play Than Just Playing
http://www.meaningandhappiness.com/
oxford-happiness-questionnaire/214/.

https://fetzer.org/sites/default/files/images/stories/pdf/selfmeasures
/SATISFACTION-Subjectivehttps://www.musictherapy.org.

https://arttherapy.org.

https://www.nctrc.org.

https://www.samitivejhospitals.com/article/detail/happiness-hormones.

https://www.youtube.com/watch?v=8KkKuTCFvzI&t=145s Robert Waldinger.
Happiness.pdf.

Oxford happiness questionnaire
http://www.meaningandhappiness.com/oxford-happiness-questionnaire
/214/.

Chapter Twelve: Embrace Your Inner Child
https://integrativepsych.co/new-blog/what-is-an-inner-child.

Chapter Thirteen: My Illusion of My Birth Mother
Davis, Shirley. "The Long-Term Effects of Abandonment" Feb 25, 2021.
Abandonment and CPTSD.

https://cptsdfoundation.org/2021/02/25/the-long-term-effects-of
-abandonment.
Ortner, Nick. *The Tapping Solution: A Revolutionary System for Stress-Free Living.* Hay House Publishing, 2013.

Chapter Fifteen: The No Contact Clause

How long does estrangement last?
https://www.psychologytoday.com/us/blog/constructive-wallow-ing/201908/how-long-does-parent-child-estrangement-usually-last.

Pillmer, Karl. Understanding Estrangement.
https://youtu.be/L75oJPFw7cU.

The plight of rejected parents
https://youtu.be/6Puy0hjtedU.

Brooks, David. "What's Ripping American Families Apart?" New York Times, July 29, 2021. https://www.nytimes.com/2021/07/29/opinion/estranged-american-families.html.

Facebook support groups:
Family estrangement support group.
Estranged Mothers Support Group.
Dr. Joshua Coleman Parent / Grand-parent Estrangement Support Group.

Chapter Sixteen: When Enough Is Never Enough

For more information about Bright Line Eating, go to brightlineeating.com.
https://www.mayoclinic.org/diseases-conditions/obesity/symptoms-causes/syc-20375742
https://www.samhsa.gov/find-help/national-helpline.
https://www.egglestonyouthcenter.org/blog/the-link-between-childhood-trauma-and-eating-disorders/.

Michael Blackstone https://michael-blackstone.mykajabi.com/
linkedin.com/in/michaelblackstone.

https://www.cdc.gov/obesity/data/adult.html.
Hyman, Dr. Mark. *The Blood Sugar Solution: The UltraHealthy Program for*

Chapter Eighteen: Anger To Peace, One Layer at a Time

https://insighttimer.com/happymindmeditation/guided-meditations/deep-sleep-meditation-528hz-miracle-tone#:~:text=Designed%20to%20help%20you%20drift,a%20special%20connection%20with%20Nature.
https://www.soulveda.com/wellbeing/sound-healing-in-ancient-egypt.

About the Author

Madison is an author, speaker, teacher, certified master life coach, reiki master, certified spiritual counselor, and certified Emotional Freedom Technique (EFT) practitioner.

As a trauma survivor, she recognizes the vital need to release past negative beliefs, emotions, and fears that cause stress, anxiety, self-doubt, and self-sabotage to live an extraordinary life of freedom. She has adapted the lessons she's learned to help others transform their lives.

For the past three decades, she has employed many different methods and techniques she learned through her studies and now uses the same methods with her clients. Madison follows her inner guidance, listens to her client's concerns, and provides a safe place to discover things within themselves that they may not have been aware of before. She is passionate about helping others in the same emotional state she was in because of all the trauma before she found her answers. She is a lighthouse shining a light on all of the rocks standing in the way for people to find a way to feel whole and become who they are.

Madison believes in giving back to her community and has served in local organizations for decades. She serves on the board of Divorce Cafe, and is a member of SHEROES United, a nonprofit organization that helps women overcome trauma. Her particular forte is working with incarcerated women who are improving their lives and desiring to leave as victors and leaders instead of victims.

Madison offers group or individual sessions. To schedule a free exploration call, go to https://www.madisonfrederick.com/

EFT certification: Awakening Institute
Master Life Coach Certification: Transformational Academy
Doterra Aroma Touch Technique ®: Certification
Feng Shui Certification: Natural Bridges Institute
Feng Shui Certification: Feng Shui For Life Mastery

Reviews

"In this book, Madison takes a brave look at her life. She revisits adversity with courage and a deep look at how the events she has experienced manifest in opportunities for her own growth. She readily admits her faults as a vehicle for evolution, and uses her introspection for creating the changes she wants in her own life. The journey and tools she shares are vulnerable and kind. Madison models a great openness to the sometimes difficult process of growth and building the life you want."
-Kara Patin LCSW
Noble Soul Therapy

"Madison Fredrick's book, Untangle the Web of Narcissism, expresses how her whirlwind romance and marriage crumbled as she reveals the trauma kept a secret for years. Her voice to the complexities surrounding the betrayal of a culture created by a narcissist. She opens her heart so we can see her pain through a mixture of emotions. Her raw honesty leads us through the journey of being raised by a narcissist, then married to one and how she broke free. She challenges us to bridge our suffering and move to a place of healing. Madison inspires us through her journey of unspeakable trauma to a place where hope emerges, and love conveys a sense of purpose."
-Maryann I Colborn, Licensed Professional Counselor
Holistic Approach Mental Health, LLC
http://www.holisticapproachmentalhealth.com/the-clinicians.html

"From the depths of despair to choosing forgiveness and love. Whether you've experienced Narcissism directly or indirectly, were raised by one, or developed coping mechanisms to survive, this book is inspiring. Madison shares her story and the path she used to overcome self-defeating beliefs and shows you how to choose a different path for yourself. As a relationship coach, reading her story of life with a partner before she really knew herself, followed by the triumph of choosing to love herself and choosing the perfect partner for her, is a case study of what's possible!"
- Kimi Avary, Relationship Navigation Specialist, Best Selling Author
https://LivingYourLifeInLove.com

"Emerging new Self-Help Author, Madison Frederick, hits a home run with Untangle the Web of Narcissism.
The book is a collection of heartfelt personal life stories – Experiences, illustrating what it is like to be on the receiving end of narcissism & gaslighting. Madison provides the tools, strategies, and modalities in each chapter to come back stronger. It is as if you are sitting down with her in a private conversation, shaking your head YES - ME TOO.
This is a book worth reading over and over again."
-Polly Fletcher
Attitude Architect, Photographer & Artist
https://instagram.com/phoebewingswanphotographer?igshid=
MzNlNGNkZWQ4Mg==

"From the first chapter to the last, this book provides a great explanation of your inner realizations and vulnerabilities, which I found extremely helpful in finding your why's and how to navigate your way in the world. I found the writing vulnerable, helpful, and very interesting content.
There is so much to learn by reading this book. Forgiveness is the mantra throughout the book. I enjoyed the read, a fantastic work by Madison Frederick."
-Ellen Havens ASN, BSN, CCTC

"If you are experiencing (or have ever experienced) narcissism in your life, then Untangle the Web of Narcissism is an important resource. Madison Frederick combines powerful and vulnerable personal stories with practical resources, tools, and techniques to help you navigate these difficult encounters and their long-reaching aftereffects. The book provides hope without downplaying the challenging journey that is necessary to recover from the emotional and mental abuse inherent in narcissistic relationships."
-Karen Ann Bulluck
Bestselling Author, Speaker, Risk-Taking Coach
Daring to Transcend
https://daringtotranscend.com

"I had no idea about Narcissism and the devastating effect it can have on a person. Through the stories, I was able to feel the pain, but also was given very helpful insight and knowledge on ways to cope and find ways to heal. Especially liked that at the end of each chapter, Madison gave the reader the opportunity to see the steps to use. I also like the quotes referenced under the chapter headings. I look forward to buying a copy!"
-Wendy Turner, Salt Lake City

"Untangling" is part memoir, part self-help, but primarily it is informative. Wrapped in narratives of personal experience, Madison introduced me to markers along her trail of healing, techniques and methods that bring peace and joy in the place of confusion. The tone throughout is warm and encouraging. She sincerely wishes each reader freedom and health."
-Kate Nash,
Language instructor
Bright Line Eating member

"Untangle the Web of Narcissism" was written in a way that I could understand Narcissism. Madison wrote about her experience with Narcissism and its effects on her and her family. This was very enlightening as I didn't understand Narcissism. This book showed what is possible to recover from the effects when a person is willing to live a different life and do the work it takes. Madison wrote a book of compassion, hope, honesty and willingness to be open and vulnerable. Thank you, Madison."
-Judy Crenshaw

NOTES